Robert A. Parrish

Details of an Unpaid Claim on France for 24,000,000 Francs

Guaranteed by the parole of Napoleon III

Robert A. Parrish

Details of an Unpaid Claim on France for 24,000,000 Francs
Guaranteed by the parole of Napoleon III

ISBN/EAN: 9783337350420

Printed in Europe, USA, Canada, Australia, Japan

Cover: Foto ©ninafisch / pixelio.de

More available books at **www.hansebooks.com**

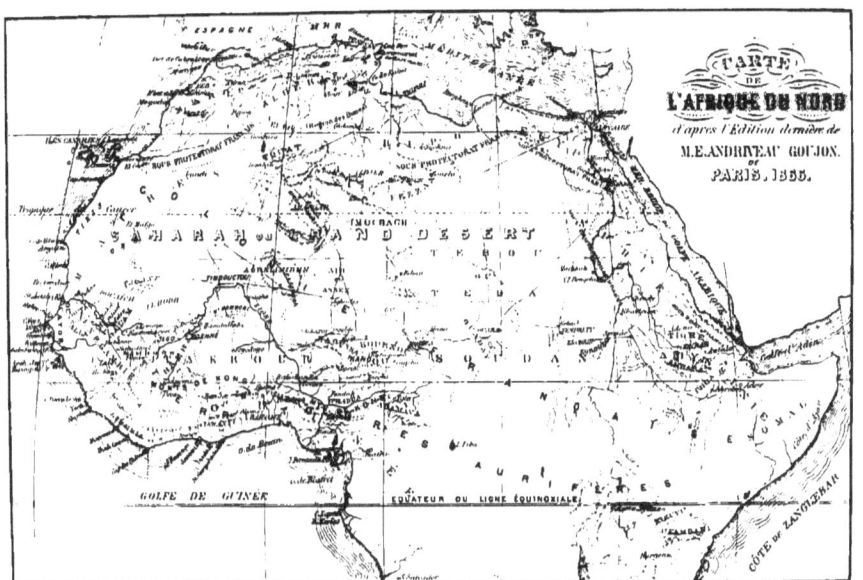

DETAILS

OF

AN UNPAID CLAIM ON FRANCE

FOR

24,000,000 FRANCS,

GUARANTEED BY THE

PAROLE OF NAPOLEON III.

TUTTI I FRANCESI SONO BURBANTI.
NO:—NON TUTTI, MA BUONAPARTE!

PHILADELPHIA:
1869.

INDEX.

Alliance of Napoleon III with the Pope and Jews............................2, 3, &c.
Africa—French Mil. Exped'ts in..9, 92-6
 Decrees relating to...........99, &c.
 Colony of Senegal............ 34-5
 Mails to..................................... 105
 Gold formations in...17-8, 86, 91
 Gold products of..9, 17-8, 91, 121, 126-7
 Value to France...............18, 93-8
 British title in North, extinguished...................13, 96, 102, 104
Address of the Emperor to Perfect of Tours.. 7
Address of the Emperor in Algeria 98
Affidavit of Capt. L. Carr............ 11
 Hon. J. T. Picket, U. S. Consul to Vera Cruz................... 20
Affidavit of Hon. S. L. Governeur, U. S. Consul to Foo Chow......... 45
Affidavit of Col. George Mackay... 55
 Donn Piatt, Esq., Secretary of Legation..................... 56
Affidavit of Dr. C. M. Wilkins...... 57
Audience of Claimant by the Emperor, (1)..................................... 22
Audience of Claimant by the Emperor, (2)..................................... 48
Audience of Claimant by Prince Napoleon................................... 131
Audience of the Claimant by Mr. Fould, (1).................................. 21
Audience of the Claimant by Mr. Fould, (2).................................. 22
Audience of the Claimant by Mr. Fould, (3).................................. 24
Audience of the Claimant by Mr. Ducos, (1).................................. 23
Audience of the Claimant by Mr. Ducos, (2).................................. 24
Audience Book at the Tuileries... 47, 63
Anglo-saxon Nations, hostility to, 3, 5-6
Army of Soudan, Surg. in Chief... 97
Arrival of Claimant in Paris, (1)... 21
 "   "   "   (2).. 21
 "   "   "   (3).. 40
Assassination of Pres't Lincoln... 8
 Mr. Morley................................. 72
 Attempts upon Claimant, 52, 58-9, 61-5, 73-4
 of Sibour, the Archbishop of Paris..............................58-9, 66-7
Assassination of a French Gen'l in the Tuileries......................... 66
Assassination of General J. A. Thomas...................................... 63
Assassination, Orsini conspiracy, A practice with the French Government................52, 58, 66, 67
Assassination in Prison at Vincennes.. 52

Arms, traffic in, Treaties regulating.. 102
Attaché to U. States Legation in Paris...................51-6, 58, 61, 71, 76-7
Argument of Claimaut on Civil and Common Law.................. 113
Argument of Claimant on International Law................................. 133

Bourgeoisie of Paris..................... 1, 2
Bambouk, Gold Mines of...18, 93-8, 101-4
 Seized by France...93-4, 101-4
Bribery of Demagogues............... 5
 Of the Empress.....107, 125-7, 129-30
 Of the Imperial Family...107, 125-7, 129-30
 13,000,000 diffused in............ 51, 130
Baron A. Rothschild..............7, 10, 73
Beaumont, Elie de........................ 97
Brodhead, Hon. R., correspond..., 20
Buchanan, villainy of..,10, 20, 50-2, 63, 67, 73, 82, 110
 Visit to, of Claimant............ 29
Bulletin, letter to Buchanan........ 67
Belmont, His Ex'y August......... 45
Bank of Senegel chartered......... 99
Brewster, Dr., ambuscade dinner. 63
Bonaparte, Prince Napoleon...7, 104, 131
Brown, John, raid of..................... 5

Claim, narrative of....................... 11
Claimant's arguments...............113, 133
 Arrivals in Paris..............21, 24, 40
 Audience by His Majesty...... 22, 48
 Prince Napoleon.............. 131
 Mr. Fould................21, 22, 24
 Mr. Ducos.................23, 24
 Character................................. 132
 Memorial.................................. 12
 Records forged.46-7, 64, 70, 108-9, 111
Col. Faidherbe's reports, &c., Gov. of Senegal........................... 92-6
Count d'Escayrac de Lauture...... 96
Cabinet Explosion in France....9, 78, 106
Clermont-ferrand, Mr. Laroche de, 97
Credit Mobilier.............7, 9, 107, 125-30
Cushing, Hon. C., letter............ 19
Carr, Capt. Lewis, affidavit........ 11
Cottaint, Mad., intrigues, &c..... 59-62
Conquests in Africa, (see Africa.)
Cass, Hon. Lewis, letter to........ 67
Cobb, Hon. Howell, correspond.... 74-5
Courts of Senegal.................103, 105
Compulsory labor in Senegal....... 101
Common law, argument on........ 113
 Civil   "   "   "   113
Collet Meygret, Rec. General disgraced...................................... 129
Count de Persigny, correspond..... 131
Court, presentation of Claimant.. 48-50
Co-partner of Claimant..........35, 36, 107

[iv]

	PAGE
Divorce of the Empress, rumor of.	128
Duke of Bassano, Grand Cham., correspondence	33
Ducos, Minister French Marine, correspondence	27
Dumont, Mad., intrigues of	50–62
Desvaux, boring Artesian Wells in the Desert	95
De Tocqueville, democracy in America	6
Demagogues, ignorance of	6, 7
Dayton, U. S. Min'r to France	10
De Richmont, Viscount, suicide	127–8
De Morny's disgrace	125–130
Debate in French Senate on the Mirés Frauds	129
Department of State, forgeries in, 46, 47, 64, 70, 108, 109, 111	
Defamation of Claimant	10, 49–50, 63–4, 73, 141-2
Decrees of the Emperor	99, &c.
De Beaumont, Elie	97
De Clermont, Ferrand	97
English title to the West Coast of Africa	13, 96, 102, 104
England, commotions in	4
Undermined by the Jews	4
And U. S. Rebellion	7
Emperor of France, address at Tours	7
Emperor of France in Algeria	98
Treaty with Jews	2
With the Pope	2–4, 6, 82
Claimant	10, 22, 25
Audiences of Claimant	22, 47-8
Letters to Claimant	33
Opinion of Claim't's Scheme	97-8
Approval of "	25–6
Empress, bribery by the Jews.	9, 107, 125
Divorce rumored	128
Elopement to Scotland	9, 107
Expelled from Councils	107, 125
French Senate, debate on Mirés Frauds	129
Fleury, Gen. in disgrace	126
Fould, Achille, threat of Louis Philippe	2
Fould, Achille, Min. of the Imp. Household, resigns	124
Fould, Achille, audiences of the Claimant	21, 22, 24
Fould, Achille, letters to Claim't	22, 33
Forgery, &c., Mirés arrested for	125
In U. S. Dept. of State	46-7 64, 70, 108-9, 111
Faidherbe, Col., Gov. of Senegal, Reports	92, &c.
Fenian Brothers	5
French conquests in N. Africa	92-6
Protectorate over "	96
Grouchy, Marshal, Portrait lacerated	1
Golden Circle, Knights of	5
Gold Mines in Africa	12, 17-8, 89, 93-4, 99, 103-6
Gouverneur's affidavit, Hon. S. L.	45
Hebrew-Papal alliance	3
Herald, N. Y., Claimant's narrative in	78
Herald, N. Y , Mirés Frauds in	125
Hayti, revolution in	3, 80-2
Jews in Mexico, Jecker claim	3
The authors of Revolution of 1848	2

	PAGE
Jews, the Bourgeoisie of Paris	2
Jomard, Vice-Pres. Geog. Society address	97
Jews in English Government	4
In Southern Confederacy	8, 10
International Sanhedrim	7
Johnson, Pres., Treason of	10
Jus Gentium, argument on	133
Ku Klux Klan, organized by France	5
Knights of the Golden Circle	5
Latin Races	3
Memorial of the Claimant	12
Ministers of France disgraced	126
Moniteur, Decrees in	99
Mocquard, correspondence	53
Monopoly of Gold Mines by Fr'e	94
Mason, Hon. J. Y., U. S. Ambassador, bribed	50, 51
Mason, Hon. J. Y., letters to	30, 47
Treason of	58
Mirés, fraud and arrest of	125-30
Morny, Count de, fraud of	125-30
Marcy, Hon. Wm. L., correspond.	61
Maygret, Collet, Receiver Gen'l, disgraced	129
Napoleon III and the Jews	2, 124-5
Parole	2, 25, 22, 113
Napoleon, Prince	7, 97, 104, 131
Niger basin of	16, 93, 95
Negro Troops in Senegal	93, 99
Negroes, compulsory labor of	101
exported as apprentices	101
emigrants	101
Pope, the agent of Revolutions	3, 80, 82
Peculation of $120,000,000!!	107, 126
Prolegomena	1
Prefect of Tours, address to	7
Prince Napoleon, audiences	131
Pope, ally of France	3, 82
Pope's Blessing on U. S. Rebellion	7
Pickett, Hon. J. T., affidavit	20
Piatt, Hon. Donn, Sec. of Legat'n.	56
Pency, Army of Soudan	97
Pellegrini, Pres. Geo. Society	96
Prussia and U. S. Rebellion	7
Rebellion instigated by France	3, 5
the Pope	7
Reports, French, of conquests,&c.	9, 92
Rabbis	7, 142
Revolution, French, of 1848	1
Rothschild, Baron A.	7, 73
Sanhedrim of Jews in Paris	7
San Domingo, Revolution in	3, 80-2
Seward, His Ex. W. H., corresp.	109-24
Stolen, $120,000,000.	107, 126
Soudan, commerce of	93, 97
French Army of	97
Capital towns of	94
Traffic in Arms in North Africa	102
Treaties with various Governm's. with England, (W. Coast)	102 102
Timbuctou, value of	18, 94
U. States, Rebellion in, origin of.	3
Victoria instigating Rebellion	7
Watts, His Ex. H. M., letter of	49
White Men not admitted to the Gold Mines	94

AMOUNT OF THE CLAIM.

Payable 15th Aug. 1854,   Frs. 15,000,000
Int. (4 per ct.) to Aug. 1869,   9,000,000

                            Frs. 24,000,000

DOCUMENTARY EVIDENCE,
IMPERIAL DECREES, CORRESPONDENCE
AND FRENCH OFFICIAL REPORTS,

Relating to a Claim for 24,000,000 Francs, of Mr. Robert A. Parrish, Jr., of Philadelphia, upon the Emperor and Government of France.

PROLEGOMENA.

The French Revolution of 1848, which in the interest of Louis Napoleon obliterated Louis Philippe, has never been ascribed to its true causes. The Histories of Europe are seldom evoked by a love of truth. Like stock-brokers' telegrams, they are the offspring of selfish interest or of sheer faction. It is admitted at all hands, however, that this popular eruption, sudden as a thunder-clap, took not only the Provinces of France, but even the City of Paris by surprise! No adequate explanatory symptoms of popular excitement existed, and nothing could have been more startling than its astonishing suddenness, except, perhaps, its organized results. The laceration of Grouchy's portrait in the Salle des Marechaux, on the occasion of the irruption of the mob into the Palace of the Tuileries, was the key-note however to the aim and import of the Revolution. From its very inception it was a Napoleonic movement, and bore upon its front the palpable badge of Faction. The people were its passive instruments and victims—not its instigators.

As soon as its primary purpose (the exile of the king) was consummated, the bourgeoisie of Paris quietly usurped the control of affairs, and gradually elevated Napoleon to his present position. The sequel is well known.

These bourgeoisie, however, are a vague and indefinite power in Paris. Whilst understood to mean what the term "solid men" means in Boston (namely, the mass of wealthy and prosperous citizens); and whilst their theoretical views and interests were then the incessant theme of the press, in point of fact, this undefined, mysterious, intangible, but powerful bourgeoisie, were plainly and simply THE OPULENT JEWS! At that period they represented an aggregate and more or less concentrated capital of two hundred millions of dollars: in other words, an absolutely irresistible power, whether in finance or politics, if exerted in any given direction. Made crafty and cautious by the persecutions of eighteen centuries, the Jews, although conscious of their might, never disclosed themselves in the progress of affairs. Their stereotyped expression was: "*We never meddle with politics.*" They quarreled, however, with Louis Philippe. At that moment his doom was sealed. Gregarious, both from instinct and necessity, they not only were accustomed to operate en masse, but, for their general security, always subsidized one of his ministry. They thus, as early as himself, knew every coming political event which could influence either the welfare of their people or the value of their stocks. The king, actuated by the cupidity of a Shylock, and with the aid of his whole official knowledge, was like themselves continually operating upon the Bourse. His attempt to cope with them was utterly futile. Exasperated at length by reiterated defeats, he protested that unless their manœuvres ceased he would transport to Algiers the ostensible offender, Mr. Achille Fould. It was this threat which cost him his throne!

Louis Napoleon was then a needy and discomfitted exile in London, forbidden the territory of France on pain of death. He was approached and sounded. The means to canvass France and reach supreme power were tendered him on condition of a cordial alliance with the Jews, giving them place in the Ministry and dominion over the Exchequer of the new Government. The Treaty was accomplished, and the revolution of 1848 was forthwith extemporized. No subsequent event either in the career of Napoleon or in the policy of France can be possibly interpreted aright, without this clue to its origin and true meaning. The menaced Mr. Achille Fould, from the outset of Louis Napoleon's career, sat at his right hand not only during the so-called Republic but during the Empire, and as Minister both of the Presidential and Imperial households was virtual keeper of the Imperial conscience. Up to the last hour of Mr. Fould's existence the correspondence of the French President and Emperor was under his absolute control. The Jews are an over-ruling power behind the throne. With the aid of the Jews that of the Pope was likewise secured for the new dynasty. These agencies operating together not only enabled Louis Napoleon to reconstruct the Map of Europe and develop our late Rebellion, *but are at this moment still insidiously working to overthrow our Republic and to imperialize America!* A newspaper in this interest has been recently established in New York.

It was the combined machinations of this Satanic trinity which overthrew the King of Naples, employing Garibaldi as their deeply deluded agent; which remodeled Germany; which overthrew the Governments of Hayti, San Domingo, and (in the pretended prosecution of the Jecker Claim) the Republic of Mexico, as preliminaries to the ephemeral Empire of Maximilian. To them also, far more potentially than to any other influence, was due the existing rebellion in Spain. Out of these vast commotions the wealth of the Jews and the power of the Pope have quadrupled. With a prescient knowledge of results they have always contrived to make war pay for war, and thus to prosper and fatten on the ruin of mankind.

Never before had the sun looked down upon such a scene of national felicity as, prior to the Rebellion of 1861, was presented to the world by the Republic of the United States. Nor, since the entrance of the Serpent into Eden, has such fiendish havoc been made as was made by that Rebellion upon the hopes of man. Under the plea of giving ascendancy to the Latin races, and consolidating the aristocratical interests of Europe, dissensions (of which this was a part) have been assiduously disseminated by Louis Napoleon, *and are still in train* amongst the dreaded Anglo Saxon nations. The fifteen thousand millions of dollars annihilated by our Rebellion is but a portion of the vast mischief which is still on foot. Since the Jews have gained access to high places in England the foundations of her political fabric also have given way, and the handwriting of coming disaster is discerned upon her walls. Like the sections of this Union before the Rebellion, England and the United States are drifting into irreconcilable collision without a suspicion by the masses of their people of the source from which the instigation comes. That collision, whilst weakness mutually to us, will be relative strength to them, as it must prodigiously contribute to the temporal power of the Pope and the financial power of the Jews. The social and political system of England, like our own, is pervaded with organized and widely ramifying influences that are slowly sapping the fountains of her vitality. Throughout England, France and the United States the newspaper press, as well as their legislative bodies, have largely succumbed to these encroachments and have *ceased to represent the people.* Corrupted by the exquisite craft and the opulence of this Napoleonic-Papal-Hebrew alliance, they have become false guides or the parricidal enemies of their constituents. The Jews and Catholics at this moment administer power, corruptly acquired, in the two largest cities in the Union.

Ignorance may deride that awful and consummate craft, which for nearly two thousand years has been acquired and practiced by the Romish Church, and which has attained for it almost unrestricted empire over the confidence of men; and may also deride the titanic energy of that craft and skill in finance, which during a still longer period has been acquired by the Jews; but both these bodies in their respective departments are profoundly wise; departments in which most other men are profoundly ignorant. It is the exercise of just such wisdom which constitutes the whole art of European government. Since their advent to power in France, as allies of the military piracy of Louis Napoleon, armed as they are with supreme wealth, they have constituted the most formidable coalition against the interests of Christendom which has ever scathed the earth. Through them, new instrumentalities, or on a larger scale than ever before, have been introduced into the arena of diplomacy—the wholesale bribery of Generals, national Chiefs, and Representative Bodies, whereby the voice of the people is annulled; the most mendacious use of the telegraph and of the public press, together with the widespread employment of secret societies. Over four hundred newspapers in the United States are under the dominion of the New York agent of the Rothschilds, who is the reigning chief of the Democratic party. They are profitable as well as powerful. During the approach and progress of the late Rebellion in the United States, the function of this branch of the American press was to exasperate and alienate the sections by an unpatriotic and an unprecedented violence of invective. Since then it has systematically advocated and legitimated treason, assassination and other cognate crimes. It has done its work effectively. The consolidation of our various telegraph companies under one general administration was an essential part of the same programme. The secret societies of the "Fenian Brotherhood," the "Golden Circle," and the "Ku-klux Klan," all of which are illegal conspiracies, largely devoted to crime, were also a part; as also were the treasonable intrigues which so widely pervaded both the army and civil service, carrying a leprous rot into the very vitals of the Republic. The selection and dispatch of John Brown upon his visionary crusade, his grand dramatic trial, the exaggerated diffusion of its details through the press, coupled with incessant and most mischievous allusions to the romance of Uncle Tom's Cabin—these and similar machinations, treacherously practiced upon the most moral and hence the least suspicious race upon the earth, (a people who suspected neither the loyalty of their churches, nor the loyalty of their partisan chiefs,) were not only the indispensable and carefully devised preliminaries to our Rebellion, but alone explain its possibility, its progress, and its wonderful success. *That it was organized in Europe, and was predicted there some years before its culmination here, is a proposition which admits of absolute proof.*

When the present French Empire was engrafted upon its assassinated republic, the press of the Anglo Saxon nations, as with one voice, broke forth into yells of furious malediction. Those of the United States were the most formidable and most unsparing. This affront was recorded by the ruffian Empire; it has since been fearfully avenged.

The ignorant demagogues who for many years had wielded unbridled control over our public affairs, took many and wanton opportunities both to insult and alarm the aristocratical governments of Europe. The affair of the Black Warrior with Spain, of Martin Kozsta and Kossuth with Austria, of the Papal Nuncio Bedini with the Pope, and the universal anathema maranatha of our press and parliamentary bodies over the Coup d'Etat in France, to say nothing of the Ostend Manifesto, may be quoted as illustrations. These mortal indignities, the less pardonable because justly grounded, were hurled at the heads of their victims in their hour of greatest tribulation, pending the continental convulsions ensuing the fall of Louis Philippe. The previous application of steam to ocean navigation had converted the Atlantic into a mere ferry, and brought the old and new worlds into close proximity; the flood of emigration to the United States, and the returning mails to Europe freighted with unceasing encomiums of the Republic, were operating silently but powerfully to strengthen a jealousy against us. If anything further were wanting to consummate the solicitude of Europe it was supplied by the publication of De Tocqueville's "Democracy in America." In short, the aristocratic and republican systems of government in all their interests had grown into an attitude of fatal antagonism. Our demagogues pushed the struggle *a l'outrance*. Self-preservation thus exacted of the governments of Europe the destruction of this Republic as the only alternative to their own annihilation. The French Imperial biographer of Julius Cæsar (who had perused and penned the fate of Carthage,) saw and accepted this necessity. Knowing that the congregated arms of Europe would be powerless against the indomitable military spirit of our people, and that failure in an armed attempt against us would be inevitable ruin, it was resolved to make us destroy ourselves! This would be a masterpiece of diplomacy! The influence of our churches, the unexampled military genius of the Republic, the blind confidence of the nation in their party chiefs, and the unchecked license of our press, were all to be employed against us. It was most successfully done. The stratagem largely succeeded, although its immediate hopes have seemed to fail. But the end is not yet. The fate of the Republic still hangs upon portentous issues unheeded by our demagogues, and which have not even been made by them the subjects of discussion. This indeed was virtually declared by the Emperor when, in view of the Mexican failure, he said in his celebrated address to the Prefect of Tours, "That notwithstanding occasional *defeats*, (for which word the press was stopped to substitute the word *checks*,) he would still persevere."

The memorable interviews of Napoleon III with the Emperor of Austria at Darmstadt, in 1858, with Queen Victoria at London, with the King of Prussia at Paris, and the notorious presentation of a cannon by that Queen to the French Emperor, were initial acts in the great tragedy of our Rebellion. It was then and there that the Rebellion was concocted. Without such inspiration it could never have existed. Eleven millions of dollars were supplied by Prussia, and a large sum by England, to be used for the purpose. The great Credit Mobilier of Paris (which was a political engine in disguise,) operated much of this fund through the Jews. Baron Anselm Rothschild visited the United States in person in 1861, followed by Prince Napoleon, to further organize the programme. An international Sanhedrim, both of Rabbis and lay Jews, convened in Paris the same year and with the same objects. By these expedients, whilst an army of European spies, agitators, and emissaries pervaded the country, and whilst the bulk of the nation were sleeping in ignorant security, our sanguinary Rebellion was precipitated upon us. To the never-ending astonishment even of its progenitors, Mr. Seward, chief of the United States Department of State, (then a mere Bureau of the French government and filled with its creatures,) actually predicted that it would endure but sixty days! And the Hebrew-Imperial alliance behind it, and the Papal benediction upon it openly and unblushingly pronounced! Well may the London Times (that grinning mask which covers the features of Louis Napoleon) declare, "The truth is, that while no people are so educated in the art and mystery of domestic government as the Americans, *no people are more ignorant of the principles of international conduct and the politics of foreign States.* The mass of the nation know nothing of the principles of government in other countries."—[Feb. 2, 1869.]

Now commenced the iniquitous harvest of the Jews, many of whom had crept into position both in the Confederate and Federal Governments. Cotton and tobacco, on a large scale, were purchased with Confederate bonds, taken (as a gracious favor to the Confederacy) at a fearful discount. Forestalling followed upon an unprecedented scale. The arms and equipments of the troops were the first subject; then iron; then coal; then leather; then gold; then real estate. Then finally wages were pushed to the vanishing point. And all this coglionerie was effectually stimulated by a perfidious employment of the press. To a scrutinizing observation throughout every stage of these events, the rancorous hatred of Napoleon III, the mischievous financial industry of the Jews, and the unappeasable malice of the Roman Catholic Church, were conspicuously visible, until at length they culminated in the assassination of President Lincoln. This thrice-heinous crime was their act. To the French Emperor and his royal confederates it was an imperious necessity. It was perpetrated wholly and solely in their interest, not in that of our rebels or of any domestic faction. As an invaluable means of promoting discord here, and of rescuing the French forces then in Mexico, especially of procuring a cordial ally in our Presidential office, this eternal infamy was positively indispensable. The assassins were all Catholics. Since the Sicilian Vespers, there has scarcely been one great political assassination in Christendom which cannot be tracked directly to the Church of Rome. *Nulla vestigia retrorsum.* The starvation of our brave and loyal soldiers in Southern prisons; the pestilential infection of our hospitals and cities;* the employment of poisoned and explosive bullets in the field; these, like the assassination of our President, are crimes familiar in practice with the Latin races, but foreign to the genius of the American people. They were imported, and were insidiously perpetrated here by our Imperial foes—ostensibly as our own acts—in order to exasperate us

---

*Vide Philadelphia Press, May 1, 1865, p. 2.

with each other. Their success has been only too triumphant. But mutually beguiled by these mournful catastrophes we may well say to our Southern friends, that in all this strife we unwittingly "have shot an arrow o'er the house and hurt our brother."

As soon as the Memorial of the Claimant (hereafter set forth,) proposing certain conquests in Africa, was surrendered to the Emperor of France, the Jews of Paris seized and appropriated its vast profits to themselves. Through the late Count de Morny (the Emperor's illegitimate brother and President of the French Senate,) the Empress and all the Imperial family were bribed, and entered as accomplices into the fraud. All approach by the Claimant to the Emperor, whether in person or by letter, was absolutely interdicted. In place of the fifteen millions of francs which the Claimant preferred to accept, the other alternative offered by the Emperor, of half the product of the African Mines, appears to have been secured by the conspirators, whilst Mirés, Chief of the Credit Mobilier, farmed out the fund. When these colossal peculations were ultimately blazoned by the Claimant through the New York Herald (Sept. 29, 1860,) the Empress was expelled from the Ministerial Councils and fled incognito to Scotland. The Count de Morny was threatened with impeachment and trial before the Legislative bodies; Mr. Mirés was arrested and imprisoned; the Bureau of the Imperial Household was abolished. Even Mr. Achille Fould retired from the Ministry! Consternation for a time presided over the Palace of the Tuileries. The Emperor found it had become a den of thieves. His own honor had been sold by the Jews for gold! The crisis, however, grew too critical. Mindful of the fate of Louis Philippe, the Emperor dared not come to open rupture with them. The Count de Morny—at least in appearance—was forgiven. Mirés, unwhipped of justice, was liberated. Mr. Fould was reïnstated in the Ministry, and the Empress was taken back to the Imperial bosom.

Meanwhile the Flag of France floated in triumph over newly conquered regions in Africa, wider and richer than extra-scythian Europe, which had been pointed out to His Majesty by the Memorial of the Claimant, and annexed to France in pursuance of its suggestions. It was then believed that the government of the United States was crumbling into ruin and would never survive to vindicate the Claimant's rights; accordingly, not a farthing of the sum for which the Imperial honor had been pledged, was allowed by these rapacious Jews to be paid to him. Mr. Mason and Mr. Dayton, our Ambassadors to France, would do for him absolutely nothing. That arch-demagogue Mr. Buchanan, late President of the United States, declared a furious war upon his interests, and not only gratuitously falsified them in many essential particulars, but authorized the outrageous corruptions practiced upon them in the United States Department of State. In fact, Mr. Buchanan acted in the premises as an advocate and agent of the French Government alone could have acted, and even mendaciously asseverated that France would resent a demand for this money BY A DECLARATION OF WAR!!

It was well known that if Mr. Lincoln had survived, this claim would have been settled. The wealth of the universe could not have bought him. The shot which closed his mortal career was no experiment; its results had all been predetermined, settled and consolidated. A well known emissary of France publicly offered his successor five hundred thousand dollars to forswear the cause of his country. Thenceforth President Johnson was a declared foe to the people of the United States, and French dictation paralysed the law of the land. When a little later the head of the French house of the Rothschilds deceased, a telegraphic message of condolence from President Johnson was dispatched to the family!

These indicial hints will serve perhaps to explain some of the delays which have beset this Claim, and to render the ensuing narrative more intelligible; a narrative which will demonstrate that Louis Napoleon, and his devoted allies the Jews, the most deadly enemies of our Republic, have not only been permitted to pillage one of its citizens on an enormous scale, but, with no nobler aim than larceny, to hunt him with assassins throughout Europe and America. Had his Claim in any interpretation been open to question, the extraordinary and costly expedients employed to defeat it would have been obviously a work of supercrogation.

NARRATIVE OF THE CLAIM,

WITH PART OF THE EVIDENCE ON FILE AT WASHINGTON.

1853, March 14th.—Mr. Parrish, the Claimant, submitted to the Government of the United States a written Memorial (now in the possession of the French Government,) proposing a military expedition to Africa, nominally to explore the valley of the Niger, but in fact also to develop the auriferous regions in the Kong Mountains on the west coast of that continent, and annex them as a colony to the United States. [Approved, but withdrawn.]

Affidavit of Lewis Carr.

Lewis Carr, of the City and State of New York, being duly sworn according to law, deposes and says:

That he resided in the City of Washington, D. C., during the winter of 1852 and 1853, at which time and place his attention was invited by Mr. Robert A. Parrish, Junior, of the City of Philadelphia, to a Proposition for the colonization and development of certain auriferous territories in Africa, in which he desired the coöperation of the Government of the United States. With that intent, this deponent called with him upon General C. Cushing, then United States Attorney General, and heard their conversation in relation thereto. It resulted in a request, on the part of the Attorney General, to receive Mr. Parrish's views in writing. Mr. Parrish accordingly prepared a written Memorial of some fifteen or twenty pages, setting forth the geology and other material facts of the case, which was delivered to General Cushing for his further consideration, who some weeks afterwards reported that, whilst admitting the facts upon which it was based, the Government was unable to coöperate in the scheme. LEWIS CARR.

Subscribed and sworn to before me, this 21st of October, 1865.
R. A. SHEWELL, *U. S. Commissioner.*

Proposition to the Government of the United States.

WASHINGTON, March 14, 1853.

SIR:—I send you in a hurried form the "Memorial" mentioned a day or two ago. If you are disposed to think well of it, be pleased to lay it before his Excellency the President.

I have the honor to be your obedient servant,
R. A. PARRISH, JR.

HON. C. CUSHING, U. S. Att'y-Gen'l

WASHINGTON, March 14, 1853.

SIR:—I beg leave to submit to the Government a Memorial proposing an expedition to the Niger, *via* Bathurst and the River Gambia. It will require equipments for one hundred men. One small vessel and a small expense will suffice. The immense national advantages to accrue from the Expedition are detailed in the Memorial herewith enclosed.

I have the honor to be your obedient servant,
R. A. PARRISH, JR.

To the President of the United States.

MEMORIAL
Proposing an Expedition to the Niger, &c.

WASHINGTON, NATIONAL HOTEL, }
March 14, 1853. }

The Kong Mountains of Africa, which extend from the 15th parallel of north latitude to the unexplored wilderness beyond the Equator, contain the richest gold deposits in the world. In the northwestern summits of the range the Senegal, the Gambia, the Rio Grande, and the Niger or Quorra take their origin. Along their southern acclivities innumerable smaller streams leap in cascades from terrace to terrace, and wander to the Atlantic through alluvial plains whose dust is gold. All of these rivers roll over golden sands. The names not only of the Gold Coast, but of the larger territory also, denominated Guinea, are derived from these well ascertained facts. On the northern side of this mountain chain lies the magnificent valley of the Niger—a stream which, after a route of two thousand miles, pours forth its flood through a hundred mouths on the coast of Calabar. Near its banks, but over a thousand miles from its mouth, is the city of Timbuctoo, equally famed for its gold mines as for the more than Indian luxuriance of the adjacent vegetation. That the mineral and agricultural wealth of the basin of this river surpasses all that the world has heretofore revealed, is conceded by every writer or traveler familiar with the subject; and if white labor and enterprise (unappalled by apprehensions of its climate,) could be induced to render it the field of their operations, not only would its opulence throw the stupendous commerce of the Indies into the shade, but would confer upon the people who controlled it a degree of prosperity as yet unexampled in the experience of nations.

The obstacles originating in considerations of climate do not oppose a substantial bar to the attainment of such a result. The existence of the gold deposits, although not yet generally known, will soon be divulged, and will inevitably be the means of transferring myriads of the Caucasian races to this region. It remains, therefore, an important question to determine whether the United States will appropriate to herself (as she may do,) the entire political fruits of this movement, or whether she will fling them a prey to the indolent cupidity of England.

In order to the acquisition of political jurisdiction over this section of Africa a variety of reasoning suggests itself. The solicitude of Great Britain, however, in regard to the slave trade, seems to furnish the most immediate and the most feasible.

The factories of Great Britain on the African coast occur from point to point from above the mouth of the Senegal (now in the hands of the French), with but little intermission, all the way down to the Cape of Good Hope. Many of them, however, as ruinous experiments, have been abandoned, and many others (which are still kept up at a great sacrifice of human life) are so severe a tax, both upon the solicitude and the treasure of the government, that they also would be abandoned with very little reluctance. The object in still retaining them originates in the vain hope that through their agency the slave trade may be ultimately extinguished. As a consideration, therefore, to England, for the surrender into our hands of the range of coast from the Senegal to the Equator, we might readily stipulate at our own expense to put a conclusive stop to the exportation of slaves within a period of ten years. Such a stipulation, whilst it left all the southern coast of the continent to the enterprising philanthropy of England, would be unaccompanied by any effort or expense to us; inasmuch as we should not only save the cost of our existing squadron on that coast, but would have to do no more in the accomplishment of the stipulation than merely to make proclamation of the existence of the mines. From the extensive immigration to this region which would immediately ensue, it is manifest that the slave trade would in a few years become *ipso facto* impossible. At least the exportation of slaves would become an impossibility, for even if the trade were still to go on, slaves would bring a better price at the mines than in any other quarter of the globe. Whatever the fate of the slaves, therefore, the treaty would be fulfilled. The cost, then, of our present squadron in those seas (which in ten years has already exceeded the sum of   millions) would thenceforth be saved to the treasury, and might fairly be diverted to the establishment of the Ebony line of steamers which has already been suggested between this country and Liberia.

Whilst the promise of such a line of steamers would furnish an additional inducement to England to hope for the realization of her anti-slavery expectations, it would at the same time operate as a wholesome sedative at home, not only by aiding to divert the filibustero feelings of "Young America" into a legitimate channel, but also by giving a practical turn to the free soil, colonization and abolition delusions so prevalent in the Northern states.

There is perhaps no common ground upon which the discordant prejudices of our country in regard to slavery would be so likely to meet and harmonize, as upon an enterprise of this very kind. With the great majority of our people colonization is the only panacea for the multifarious evils which surround the question of slavery. It would be listened to in all quarters. It would sanctify almost any project and justify any reasonable degree of expenditure. In England, at the same time, it is the hobby of that whole school of transcendental philanthropists who have nearly converted the British Parliament into a Camp Meeting, and who, under the plea of humanity, have ruined some of her most prosperous colonies and have forever checked the growing civilization of her slaves. In evidence of the justice of this view of the subject reference may be made to the general tenor of the debates in the British Parliament, and to the voluminous proceedings of the colonial and anti slavery conventions in that country for many years back. Amongst others, Sir Wm. Gore Ouseley, (late British Minister to La Plata,) has written and spoken with warmth to the same effect. In his published work entitled, "Notes on the Slave Trade," he strongly recommends the colonization of Africa as the only proper mode of disposing of liberated slaves, &c. He says, "I am possibly unduly biased in favor of the plan of sending all liberated Africans to our colonies, as I was the first to recommend and adopt that mode of providing for them, &c.," p. 72. He even goes so far as to promise the coöperation of Brazil in his colonization scheme, saying that "at a former period the Brazilian Minister had himself proposed thus providing for the Negroes," p. 72. Sir Harry Huntley, at one time colonial Governor of Gambia, further adds, " As for the squadron suppressing the Slave Trade when four hundred per cent. is to be realized upon money invested in it, the thing is nonsense," Slave Coast, p. 20. * * "It is idiocy if not treachery to talk of the Slave Trade being put down by the squadron, numerous as it is," ibid. p. 21. * * "It is an admitted maxim that wherever a thing is produced, a demand will always be followed by a supply. Is not this maxim to extend to the Slave Trade, with its superior remuneration, as well as to other trades?" Ibid. p. 22.

The English colonies on this coast (if such they can be called,) are usually known by the names of the Gambia, Sierra Leone, Cape Coast Castle, Accra, Dix Cove, Annamaboa, and Fernando Po; most of the latter lying along the grain, ivory, gold and slave coasts, or the Bights of Biafra and Benin. Fernando Po is an island immediately under the line. From the beginning they have been with slight exception mere trading posts, not aiming at political aggrandizement. The coast for a thousand miles below Cape de Verde was once interspersed with like settlements from Spain, Portugal, Denmark, France, etc.—about forty in all. Whilst the slave trade was tolerated it constituted their principal business, and they were then little else than mere barracoons. In the lapse of time, as this commerce ceased to be legitimate, nearly every one of them beyond the Senegal got little by little into the hands of the English. In 1821, the dominion over them, which had been wielded by the "African Company," was usurped by the British crown, and has been thus held (save a brief concession to a new company, beginning in 1827,) until the present time. A Colonial Governor at Sierra Leone presides over the whole, with Lieutenant Governors at each of the principal points. In the year 1833, they cost in all forty thousand pounds beyond their revenues and they are believed never to have supported their own expenses. Of late years they have done a little better; but many of the factories have been abandoned in despair. Their total cost to England from 1750 to 1830 was over £8,000,000 sterling—"a prodigality of expenditure unmatched," as McCulloch has it, "except by its uselessness." In spite of the efforts of the government to suppress the slave trade even by an extension of the factories some fifteen years ago, it has still continued to prosper, and the hoped for project of its extinction has totally failed.

Sir Harry Huntley also says: "The whole attempt is a melancholy failure. Melancholy because the best hopes of excellent men have been frustrated; and because it has been *fully proved* that, as yet, the endeavor of England to extend Christianity and civilization into Africa has only resulted in an enormous loss of life, talent and treasure."—Vol. I, p. 23.

So settled is the conviction of the utter futility of these endeavors, that McCulloch goes so far as to treat it thus: "As a means of checking the prevalence of the illicit slave trade, the establishment of a colony at Sierra Leone has been worse than useless. ..... Blacks may be advantageously employed to fill the official situations in the colony; but even if otherwise, it ought to be *unconditionally abandoned.*"—McCulloch's Com. Dic., Vol. II, p. 484.

The aggregate cost to the English Government of these colonies now averages about forty thousand pounds per annum, exclusive of the enormous off-shore expenses connected with the squadron. They are with slight exception purely trading posts. They neither exercise nor contemplate a political jurisdiction beyond what is necessary to the security of their local commerce.

But the purpose of this proposition is not limited merely to the jurisdiction of the African *coast*. If a treaty with England, as above suggested, should be found practicable, and a missionary settlement, with a single gun, were to be made near Atta, upon the island of Bird Rock, where the Kong Mountains cross the Niger, and below the confluence of the Tchadda, the navigation of that river might be effectually controlled.

This arrangement would give the United States a quasi jurisdiction over the whole valley of the Niger, and in connection with its authority upon the coast would warrant it in assuming dominion *between the 5th and 15th parallels of north latitude, all the way from the Atlantic to those distant highlands which divide the basin of the Niger from the basin of the Nile:*—in other words, over the only portion of Africa which would be intrinsically worth possessing.

The tax upon England for the support of her African squadron is far greater than to us. In addition to which, and in pursuance of the aristocratic and expensive system of her government, she has on shore a swarm of officers at every available post, eating up its substance, and wasting annually ten per cent. of the lives of the entire colonial corps! This disproportion between the salaries and resources of these British factories is not the only absurdity attending the system. Established as they all are on the very margin of the sea, in the most pestilential positions which ingenuity could have sought out, they have given such a reputation for insalubrity to the African continent as to have constituted it a bugaboo to the civilized world. So far, however, from the health of the interior resembling that of the coast, there is the very highest authority for asserting that it is altogether the reverse. The continent is composed of vast plateaux, elevated to a great distance above the level of the sea, and presenting a spectacle of salubrity quite unusual for tropical regions. Malte Brun, in his Universal Geography, says in this connection : "Perhaps we should not deviate far from the truth if we were to venture the assertion that the whole body of the African Mountains forms one great plateau, presenting towards each coast a succession of terraces. This nucleus of the African continent seems to contain few long and high ranges in the interior, so that if the sea were to rise *three or four miles* above its present level, Africa, stripped of all the low lands which line its shores, would perhaps appear almost a level island in the midst of the ocean."—Vol. II, p. 417, ed. 1837.

Moreover, the English Colonial Governor of the Gambia says: "Altogether, I cannot but consider it very extraordinary that this colony should have existed so long and so little as yet be known of the course of the Gambia...... But I think that having made three expeditions beyond Barraconda [head of tide navigation,] and returned without incurring any considerable danger or inconvenience, it does not appear that much expense or danger would attend such an expedition if taken at the proper season, viz: the end of December or beginning of January. I and my party *bivouacked fifteen nights in the woods and returned in perfect health.* The abundance of game to be found in the country would insure provisions—the carriage of which is in all such undertakings a great difficulty. In proof of the abundance of game I may mention that I and my party shot several elephants, numbers of deer, river horses and Guinea fowls, though we did not seek particularly for game, nor leave the banks of the river for that purpose."—p. 203, London 8vo., 1851. * * * * * *

If, then, gold exists here of a purity and in a profusion surpassing that of California and Australia; and if it be also true that the unhealthfulness of Africa is chiefly confined to the coast, and even there is limited to certain periods of the year, it is inevitable that the flood of emigration now bent toward Australia would prefer a journey of less than half the distance, particularly where it was accompanied with less than half the peril.

In the *Gazetteer of the World,* a work published lately by a member of the Royal Geographical Society, under the head of Guinea, is the following language: "The mountains of Guinea as far as they have been examined . . . . abound in veins of gold and iron. The natives in digging for gold work downwards as if forming a well, or sometimes a ditch about twenty or thirty feet deep, till stopped by the crumbling down of the earth. They generally begin *to find gold at a depth of three feet.* Pieces are sometimes found of a considerable size. The King of Ashantee is said to possess A LUMP OF NATIVE GOLD SO LARGE THAT FOUR MEN WERE REQUIRED TO LIFT IT. The earth thrown out is carried to the nearest river. The slaves of the King of Ashantee in 1790 agreed to supply him with *half an ounce per day for each laborer.* The gold finders who wash on the banks of the river and the sea shore are less successful; but the precious metal, *it is sufficiently ascertained, is very abundant in the interior of the country,* while the mines may be considered as still virgin mines." Vol. III, p. 749.

Ibid., article Gambia, "The gold of the Gambia is much softer and said to be superior to that of the leeward coast. That from Bondon, Kaarta, Manding, and the mines of Brooka and Bambarra is considered the purest." [i. e. 24 carat.]

Mungo Park says, "In every part of Manding, between longitude 8° and 9° west, and 12° and 14° north, over 7000 square miles, gold exists in large quantities." The King appoints an annual washing beginning in December. "The pit is dug with small spades or corn paddles, and the earth is drawn up in calabashes, ... for the women to wash." Harper's Family Lib., p. 41.

Park saw a woman washing gold near Shrondo, (in Bambouk.) "She put in as nearly as I could guess," he remarks, "about two pounds of gravel from a heap, and having washed it about two minutes found no fewer than twenty-three particles, some of them very small. She assured me that they sometimes found *pieces of gold as big as her fist.*" Ibid., p. 183.

Malte Brun remarks: "Amongst the objects most worthy of attention are the gold mines, which are said to exist in the country of Bambouk, situated between the Senegal and the Gambia, at equal distances between the two rivers. If we believe two French writers, Pelays and David, who were sent into this country by the old French Indian Company to examine the mines, they are situated near the villages of Natakon, Semayla, Nambia, and Kombadyree. But these grounds from which the Negroes obtain gold are only alluvial deposits derived from real mines, concealed among the mountains of Tabaoora. Eighty pounds of crude mixed earth, taken from a pit in the small mountains of Natakon, yielded one hundred and forty-four and a-quarter grains of gold. The Semayla mine appears to be the richest. There are also gold mines on the Gold Coast of Akim, five days' journey from the Danish Fort of Christianborg, but they are not very productive. At a distance of twelve days' journey further north, near the *Mountains of Kong*, we have reason to believe that the natives work a rich mine of this precious metal in the form of deep pits. .... Labat saw whole mountains of pure red marble with white veins."—Auriferous Quartz.—Geog., Vol. II, p. 518.

In Murray's Encyclopedia of Geography is the following: "The Kingdom of Bambouk is almost entirely a country of mountains, whence flow numerous streams, *almost all of which roll over golden sands.* But the main depositories, where the metal is traced, as it were, to its source, are two mountains, Natakon and Semayla. The former composes *almost an entire mass of gold,* united with earth, iron, or emery. ..... The pieces become large as the works descend. In the mountain of Semayla the gold is imbedded in hard sandstone, which must be reduced to powder before the extrication can be effected. It is also found in red marble.—Vol. III, p. 42.

Art. Timbuctoo.—"The gold mines found to the south of the river belong to the King. So rich are these mines that pieces weighing several ounces are frequently found. It is no wonder, then, that this metal should be so little prized at Timbuctoo, and that objects that are of so little value amongst Europeans, as salt, tobacco, etc., are exchanged for their weight in gold."—Malte Brun, Vol. III, p. 8.

But further argument on this point is unnecessary. It would be equally superfluous also to enter into a detail of the many and obvious reasons of a high national character which would render the territorial acquisition, here forshadowed, one of most momentous consequence to the future power and prosperity of our country.

The conspicuous ascendancy of the American Marine is to be traced directly to the necessities of our geographical position, which from the beginning drove us forth upon the sea, as upon our natural domain. The maritime habits thus engendered have developed for us a panoply of indomitable strength, which for all time must prove the future reliance of the nation in seasons of emergency. It is the peculiar felicity of our condition that this great interest may be fostered by the pacific culture "of the vast interests of commerce," and in the prosecution of the "advantages of trade and international intercourse."

To such a people who can measure the immensity of such an acquisition? What the Indias, both East and West, have already been to other powers, Africa, under a judicious policy, may be to us; and even more. The soil of this virgin continent, teeming with mineral wealth and pregnant with the perpetual presence of the sun, is destined to contribute more to the future happiness and consequent civilization of mankind than any other portion of the earth. Agriculture, navigation, commerce, scientific research—all seem waiting for its grand development to commence their respective careers of true usefulness and glory. Before the prophetic vision of a statesman a noble field is here unveiled—a future full of splendor and full of power, in whose contemplation, and with an unexaggerated enthusiasm, he may indeed exclaim—novus sæclorum nascitur ordo. R. A. PARRISH, Jr.

Gen. C. Cushing to Mr. Parrish.

WASHINGTON, 15th April, 1857.

SIR:—In reply to your note of the 7th, I state—that in the Spring of 1853 you communicated to me a Memorial, on the subject of a proposed Expedition to the River Niger and the West Coast of Africa.

Capt. Carr accompanied you, but the Memorial, I think, was in your handwriting, and I supposed the suggestions to be yours.

I conceived that the Government could not participate in the proposed Expedition; and this not only because of constitutional reasons, as indicated in your note, but for others of expediency and public policy; and the Memorial was returned to your hands. I am, respectfully,
  C. CUSHING.
R. A. PARRISH, Jr., Esq.

Letter of Hon. R. Brodhead, U. S. Senate.

PHILADELPHIA, Jan. 14, 1858.

MY DEAR SIR,—In reply to your note of yesterday's date, I have to say, that I distinctly recollect, that in the Spring of 1853, you more than once mentioned to me the subject of developing new gold fields in Africa, asserted your conviction that gold could be found there; urged the importance of the enterprise to our Government; exhibited a Memorial which you had addressed to President Pierce upon the subject, and before you left Washington, in the early part of the Summer of that year, you informed me that as our Government had declined to join you in the enterprise, you had determined to submit the same to the Government of France or some other European Power.

Truly your friend,
RICHARD BRODHEAD.
To ROBERT A. PARRISH, JR.

Certificate of Hon. J. S. Yost, late U. S. Marshal.

PHILADELPHIA, 5th January, 1858.

MY DEAR SIR,—In the Summer of 1853 you did me the great kindness of giving me a letter of introduction to the Hon. James Buchanan, (then our newly appointed Minister Plenipotentiary to Great Britian,) and thought of accompanying me on my visit to Wheatland, but were prevented.

Wishing to keep a memorandum of this fact, will you be good enough to verify this, my recollection of it?

I have the honor to be yours very truly,
R. A. PARRISH, JR.
JACOB S. YOST, ESQ., U. S. Marshal, Philada.

The above is correct. J. S. YOST.

Affidavit of the Hon. John T. Pickett, late United States Consul at Vera Cruz.

John T. Pickett being duly sworn according to law deposes and says:

That he has been acquainted with the above named Claimant since the year 1849, and being in the City of Washington in the early part of the year 1853, was made acquainted with the fact that the said Claimant had submitted to the Government of the United States a written proposition to colonize certain auriferous territories situated in Africa. After this proposition was withdrawn, (for reasons not known to this deponent,) from the Government of the United States, an effort was made by the Claimant to organize a private company, the deponent being invited to take an interest in such company. This object appears to have been thwarted by some real or supposed unfairness of one of the parties engaged in the matter, which had almost resulted in a personal conflict. After the organization of the private enterprise was abandoned the Claimant informed this deponent and others of his purpose of proceeding to Europe, with a view to lay the scheme before the Emperor Napoleon, or to invite to it the attention of some other European Government. Here this deponent's knowledge of the matter ended, as not a great while afterwards the Claimant left for Europe, and this deponent became a resident of Mexico, and it was not until the year 1858 that they again met, which was in the City of Washington, at which time the deponent received from the Claimant a full account of his negotiations with the French Government, which, for reasons not fully understood by the deponent, seemed to have been fruitless. Subsequently, namely, in the winter of 1859–60, the deponent (having always had confidence in the capacity of the Claimant to reason and act intelligently, in matters of the nature of the scheme in question, and having every reliance in his integrity and good faith,) cheerfully coöperated with others in an effort to secure the intervention of the Government of the United States in his behalf, with a view to a settlement of his said claim; which effort proved unavailing.

JOHN T. PICKETT.

Sworn and subscribed before me, this first day of April, A. D., 1867.
[L. S.]
N. CALLEN,
Notary Public.

1853, Oct. 16th.—Pursuant to his declared purpose to that effect the Claimant arrived in Paris.

First Audience of the Claimant by the Minister of the Imperial Household.

1853, October 25th.—The Claimant was received in special audience by His Excellency M. Fould, Minister of the Imperial Household, to whom he explained the object of his interview, saying that it was the same submitted to the Government of the United States, that he desired to enlist in its prosecution some of the Governments of Europe, &c. M. Fould promised to learn the Emperor's views and report.

1853, Oct. 29th.—A letter from M. Fould was received by Claimant asking another interview, viz:

Letter from His Excellency, the Minister of State and of the Imperial Household, to Mr. Parrish. [No. 1.]—*Translation.*

CABINET OF THE MINISTER OF STATE
AND OF THE IMPERIAL HOUSEHOLD,
PARIS, October 29, 1853.

MY DEAR SIR,—I desire to resume the conversation we had together a few days since, and will be obliged to you to take the pains to call on me, either this evening between six and seven o'clock, or to-morrow morning at ten.

Many compliments, &c.,
ACHILLE FOULD.

Second Audience, ibid.

1853, Oct. 30th.—Pursuant to said letter the Claimant was received in special audience again by M. Fould, at his Ministry, who reported that His Majesty would entertain the proposition and would receive the Claimant the same day at the Palace of St. Cloud, in extraordinary audience. M. Fould was reminded, as at the first interview, that unless the Emperor *would give his Parole* for the payment to the Claimant of such a sum as might be agreed on, it would be unnecessary to give him the trouble of this audience.

Extraordinary Audience of the Claimant by the EMPEROR.

1853, Oct. 30th.—His Majesty, the Emperor of France, received the Claimant in Extraordinary Audience, at the time and place appointed, and having heard the principal details of the proposition, promised to pay him *the sum of Fifteen Millions of Francs as soon as the authority of France should be established in any portion of the indicated territory;* or, if preferred, one-half the product of the mines for a term of years. His Majesty, moreover, promised the Claimant a written Treaty, to be executed by the Minister of the French Marine, to whom its further proofs as well as the execution of the scheme were referred.

His Majesty asked Mr. Parrish if he had been to Africa; if he would be willing to accompany the military Expedition to be dispatched thither: if there would not be diplomatic obstacles: whether he thought native blacks necessary adjuncts of the Expedition: what number of troops would be necessary, &c., &c. To which the Claimant responded that he had not

*Cabinet
du Ministre d'État
et de la
Maison de l'Empereur*

Mon cher monsieur,

Je voudrais reprendre la conversation que nous avons eue ensemble il y a quelques jours, et vous serai obligé de vouloir bien prendre la peine de venir me voir ce soir entre dix et onze heures ou demain matin à 10 h. ½

Mille compliments
bien dévoués

29 octob. 1853.   Achille Fould

been to Africa, and took pleasure in demonstrating these geological truths, not upon his own allegations, but upon the testimony of travelers whose integrity was unimpeachable; that he would not accompany the Expedition from choice, but would go if it were deemed necessary; that, in his judgment, a thousand well armed men could traverse that part of Africa on any diameter, but that, out of proper caution, two thousand would be more appropriate; that blacks would be indispensable; and that no diplomatic impediments were likely to arise, &c.

The Claimant further stated, that half the product of the mines would far surpass the wants of any private person—but in case he should decide to accept this alternative, that in making their computation, the cost of the Expedition should be excluded, lest they should exceed the receipts, particularly if a war with the natives should ensue, which might consume also the whole of the term of years in question. This the Emperor agreed to, and made no intimation that the territory mentioned, then, or ever, had belonged to France, or that the Scheme was not new, original, and fully worth to France all that he promised for it, or even more; the valuation thus fixed on it being his own. No sum could now re-purchase it from France.

First Audience by the French Minister of Marine.

1853, Nov. 1.—The Claimant was received in special audience by Mr. Ducos, at the Ministry of the French Marine, and gave him the original Memorial above mentioned, with other written testimony relating to the subject. The French official maps of this part of Africa were produced, the gold bearing territories pointed out to the Minister, their proper approaches, and the boundaries of the French jurisdiction in Africa discussed, and the subject left to his further consideration.

During November and December, 1853, a friend of Mr. Fould repeatedly solicited of the Claimant permission to appear as his associé in the Treaty, which was never assented to. The Claimant's power of attorney was also strenuously solicited and declined, whereupon his letters and remittances from America immediately ceased to reach him through the mails, and many formidable prosecutions beset him.

Second Audience by the Minister of the Marine.

1853, Dec. 5.—His Excellency, the Minister of the Marine, gave the Claimant another audience, saying amongst other things that the Proposition had been adopted by the Emperor, that an Expedition was then fitting out for its prosecution, and that the Treaty would be ready for execution in a few days, the delay which had already occurred being chargeable to the incessant demands upon his time by the details of the Expedition. He also said he would not pretend to disguise the importance attached to the subject, and that the Emperor evinced a renewed interest in it within a few days. He further said in reply to the Claimant's interrogation that he would not be required to accompany the Expedition to Africa.

Third Audience by the Minister of the Imperial Household.

1853, Dec. 16.—His Excellency, Mr. Fould, received the Claimant in audience, and in reply to his inquiries said, "he knew absolutely nothing of the subject since its reference to Mr. Ducos."

1853, Dec. 17.—The Claimant departed to Italy to procure other funds, his American remittances being cut off, requesting to be recalled by telegraph when Mr. Ducos was ready to execute the Treaty.

1854, May 8.—The Claimant returned to Paris, and wrote to His Excellency, Mr. Fould, as follows:

From Mr. Parrish to His Excellency, Mr. Fould, Minister of State.

PARIS, May 17, 1854.
No. 6 au Rond Point des Champs Elysées.

SIR:—I take occasion to apprise Your Excellency of my return to Paris, and of the fact that all amicable relations between Mr. ——— and myself are henceforth suspended. In connection, therefore, with the proposition I had the honor of submitting to His Majesty "for the extension of the flag of France over the gold regions of Africa," I have respectfully to request that the future communications of the Government should be addressed to myself alone.*

Whilst expressing to Your Excellency my admiration of the

---

*One of His Excellency's letters to the Claimant came through this third party.

policy—wise, comprehensive and energetic—which His Majesty has thought proper to adopt in regard to it, I cannot withhold my congratulations upon the conspicuous success with which that policy has been crowned.

For urgent reasons (which I am prepared to state, if requested,) I have further to request that Your Excellency will solicit for me another audience of His Majesty, at the earliest moment that his condescension and your own indulgence will allow.

With sentiments of distinguished consideration, I have the honor to be your obedient servant.

ROBERT A. PARRISH, Jr.

To His Excellency,
M. ACHILLE FOULD, Minister of State, Paris.

1854, May 29.—The Claimant wrote to His Excellency, Mr. Ducos; received his reply June 2d, and wrote twice to him afterwards, Paris, 1st June, and Havre, 4th July, but meantime had received a further letter from Mr. Fould of 27th June, 1854, viz:

Mr. Parrish to the Minister of the Marine. [*No.* 1.]

PARIS, May 29th, 1854.

SIR:—In the month of October last I had the honor of submitting to His Majesty in person a proposition for annexing to France a new colony abounding in gold; a colony, whose position seemed to indicate no insuperable difficulty, either of access or acquisition, and in relation to whose acquisition no diplomatic impediments were imagined to exist. The proposition was deemed to possess profound importance. Upon the consideration, therefore, that I should possess his government of evidence demonstrative of the geological value of the region, and of the feasibility of the scheme of its annexation to France, His Majesty made me an offer of fifteen millions of francs, "or one-half the profits of such mines as might be discovered, for a term of years." It was further expressly stipulated between His Majesty and myself, that if, upon an exploration, France should find reason to hoist her flag over the region in question, such fact should be taken as a "fulfillment of terms upon my part and entitle me to the consideration." It was, moreover, plainly stated, and so understood by me, in case I should decide to accept the alternative of half the profits, "that in the computation of the profits the expenses of the government should not be comprehended."

Upon this understanding His Majesty informed me that the future negotiations upon the subject should be referred to Your Excellency, who would receive and examine my proofs, and in the event of their making out such a prima facie case as to

4

Ministère
de la Marine
et des Colonies.

Direction
des Colonies.

Bureau
du Régime Politique et
du Commerce.

NOTA: Les réponses doivent être adressées
au Ministre et portes en marge l'indication
ci-dessus.

Projet d'exploitation de mines d'or
dans la Haute Sénégambie.

Paris, le 7 juin 1854.

Monsieur, Par lettre du 29 mai, vous m'avez demandé quelle suite a été donnée à vos propositions relatives à l'exploitation de mines d'or dans la Haute Sénégambie.

J'ai l'honneur de vous faire connaître que votre projet a été, de ma part, l'objet d'un examen immédiat; et qu'au mois de décembre dernier, j'ai adressé à M. le Ministre d'État et de la maison de l'Empereur, une lettre contenant, avec mon avis sur la portée et la valeur de cette proposition, l'exposé des conditions dans lesquelles il faudrait se placer pour que l'exécution en fût possible.

Je viens d'écrire à M. le Ministre d'État pour lui rappeler cette communication.

Recevez, Monsieur, l'assurance de ma parfaite considération.

Le Ministre, Secrétaire d'État, de la Marine et des Colonies.

Théodore Ducos

The Minister of the French Marine to Mr. Parrish.

"G.   PARIS, le 2 Juin, 1854.
"Ministère de la Marine et des Colonies.
"Direction des Colonies.
"Bureau du Regime Politique et du Commerce.
"*Nota.*—Les responses doivent etre adressées au Ministre, et porter en marge l'indication ci-dessus.
"Projet d'Exploitation de Mines d'Or dans la Haute Senegambie.

"MONSIEUR:
"Par lettre du 29 Mai vous avez demandé quelle suite a ete donnée a vos propositions relatives à l'Exploitation de Mines d'Or dans la Haute Senegambie. J'ai l'honneur de vous faire connaitre que votre projet a ete de ma part, l'objet d'un examen immediat, et qu au mois de December dernier j'ai adressé à Mr. le Ministre d'Etat et de la Maison de l'Empereur, une lettre, contenant avec mon avis sur la portée et la valeur de cette proposition, l'exposé des conditions, dans lesquelles, il faudrait se placer, pour que l'execution en fut possible.
"Je viens d'ecrire, à Mr. le Ministre d'Etat pour lui rappeler cette communication.
"Recevez, Monsieur, l'assurance de ma parfaite consideration.
          "THEODORE DUCOS,
"Le Ministre Secretaire d'Etat de la Marine et des Colonies.
"A Monsieur PARRISH,
          "à Paris."

Transl(

"G.   "PARIS, June 2d, 1854.
"Ministry of the Marine and Colonies.
"Direction of the Colonies.
"Bureau of Politics and Commerce.
"Project for the Development of Gold Mines in Upper Senegambia.
"*Note.*—Replies should be addressed to the Minister, and bear the above marginal indication.

"SIR:—
By letter of 29th May you have inquired what action was taken on your propositions relating to the development of gold mines in Upper Senegambia. I have the honor to apprise you that your project was the subject of an immediate examination on my part, and that in December last I addressed to the Emperor a letter containing, with my judgment of the extent and value of that proposition, an exposé of the conditions within which we must be placed, in order to render its

execution feasible. I have just written to Monseigneur, the Minister of State, reminding him of this communication.

"Receive, Sir, the assurance of my perfect consideration.

"THEODORE DUCOS,

"*Minister, Secretary of State for the Marine and Colonies.*"

To the Minister of the Marine. [*No.* 2.]

Paris, June 6th, 1854.

Sir:—Whilst acknowledging the receipt of Your Excellency's letter of the second instant, I will take occasion to express my regret that it was not as explicit upon one point as I had reason to desire. Your Excellency was silent upon the subject of the Traité. In view of the extensive action taken by His Majesty's Government since my proposition was submitted— by the recruiting of blacks in the military service of Senegal; by the dispatch of a small fleet and an exploring force to that colony; by the creation of a bank there; the reorganization of the medical corps; the establishment of a Colonial Board; the prohibition of slavery, and many other measures which have a less *obvious* connection with the subject—I feel altogether warranted, even apart from intelligence reaching me from a high quarter, in the opinion that as early as December last my proposition met with all the approval necessary as a preliminary to the execution of the Traité. If I do not err, therefore, in these impressions, will Your Excellency hold me excused if, in consideration of the disastrous effects I suffer from delay, I invite your attention now to the subject of the Traité, and request that I may be honored with a copy of it, as it is proposed to be drawn, at your earliest leisure? I deem it also proper to state that I personally waive the alternative of "half the profits of the mines," preferring that the consideration named in the Traité should be simply the sum propounded by His Majesty, of fifteen millions of francs.

On reverting to the imperial decree of the third of December last, I find it impossible to doubt that at that early date His Majesty's Government had determined upon unhesitating action upon my Proposition. And whilst it is unquestionable that to any scholar my Memorial was an all-sufficient key to the subsequent truths of the case, yet, as I have stated in a letter since written to my own Government, "it was submitted merely as the basis of a Traité, and not as a final dismissal of the subject from my hands. This is the more true from the fact that the Memorial in question was never intended for its present destination. It was a mere impromptu, written at Washington shortly after the library of Congress had been burnt, and at a time when that city contained but few authorities necessary to the elucidation of the subject. I could, therefore, if permitted, have given a much greater fullness of demonstration to its details, and could even have pointed out the very Bureau of His Majesty's Government, upon whose shelves had reposed, for over one hundred years, some of the most convincing evidence the subject admits of. I am justified, therefore, in the assumption, brief as was the array of facts contained in my Memorial, that from the silence of the French Government, they were esteemed sufficient for the demonstration of the entire subject, and that without further appeal of any kind to me, the Government felt that it already had access to all the intelligence it could desire." Indeed, so confident was I that a further demand would be made upon that knowledge of the subject with which years of study had invested me, that I have held in reserve until this hour a suggestion, which, if known, would save the Government from fifty to one hundred millions of francs; a suggestion which, from all I have been able to gather of the legislation and action of the Government, has totally escaped its attention, and which is five times more important and valuable than the entire sum it has promised to pay me.

Since the times of Pelays and David no rational scheme has ever been devised for the conquest of this region; and although many travelers, both before and since their day, demonstrated its inestimable wealth, they were dismissed one after another as unworthy of confidence, and have thus through their successive condemnation involved the subject in almost irretrievable discredit. Even Mollien, Golberry and Mungo Park published their accounts in vain. In fact, it was not until the great practical genius of the American people had demonstrated, in 1818, that a metal so precious as gold *could* occur in great masses, diffused over an extensive region, that His Majesty's Government, or any other Government, was prepared to give a serious credence to the fact. The very circumstance of the proofs in this case having been before the world for so many centuries, being found in every library, and even in the elementary geographies of schools, was enough with superficial reasoners to condemn the whole scheme. So true is this, that from 1848, when I first stirred in the matter, I have felt it sensibly at every turn. But after long delay, and much discouragement, and great tenacity of purpose, and after the President of the United States had declined to coöperate with me, through a deficiency of constitutional authority, I have at length rescued the subject from the enormous mass of prejudice under which it labored, and as I have good reason to believe, rendered my demonstrations in regard to it conclusive to the Government of France. And let me here beg Your Excellency to understand that I consider my Proposition to be a *large and valuable property;* the more, as I have been enabled to offer it to France only after very great sacrifices, both pecuniary and personal. Not only has it cost me already over twenty thousand francs; not only have I devoted to it long and laborious study, which required the application of more than one language and more than one science; but, to say nothing of over four thousand miles of travel anterior to my arrival in France, if I had not at one time drawn largely upon my personal courage, and even staked my life in its defence, I should have been pillaged of the whole enterprise long ago, and thus have given to France no opportunity of enriching herself with the fruits of my research. Estimating the matter in this light, and unwilling to lose my dominion over it on any consideration less than His Majesty's Parole, it was for this express reason that before I sought an audience, I told His Excellency the Minister of State not to give His Majesty the trouble of receiving me, "unless His Majesty were prepared to make an offer to which I could listen."

With reference to Your Excellency's Exposé as mentioned in your letter of the second instant, permit me respectfully to request that Your Excellency will not send me a copy of it nor a copy of any other document from the office of His Excellency the Minister of State, and of the Household of the Emperor, of a later date than the first day of November, 1853. This request is based upon very serious reasons, which, if desired, I will disclose either to Your Excellency or to His Majesty; a compliance with which request I conceive to be due to me as a measure of justice.

I have the honor to be with distinguished consideration and respect, Your Excellency's Most Obedient Servant,

R. A. PARRISH, JR.

To his Excellency,
THEODORE DUCOS, Minister, &c., &c., Paris.

1854, June 1.—The claimant wrote to the Ambassador of the United States, (then acting in the interest of Mr. Fould,) who made no reply, viz:

Mr. Parrish to His Excellency, Mr. Mason, U. S. Ambassador.

PARIS, *June 1, 1854.*

SIR,—The enclosed, (No. 1,) which is a copy of a letter sent by me, a day or two ago, to His Excellency the Minister of the French Marine, contains the narrative of a negotiation, beginning some months back and still pending, between myself and the French Government. Its magnitude and importance are such as to have engaged not only the excited attention of the Ministry, but also that of the Emperor himself. His Majesty's *Parole*, indeed, has been distinctly pledged to me for his Government, touching my rights in the premises, and accordingly I cannot, and do not, doubt that all the terms of that pledge will be ultimately fulfilled. There is, however, an indication, (which I may possibly have misconstrued,) of a disposition on the part of his Ministers, to delay, if not altogether to ignore me; and, taking prompt alarm at this, I have deemed it advisable, by giving Your Excellency official knowledge of the facts, to tear off at once from the transaction that veil of secrecy, in which, for the strongest reasons, it has been heretofore involved.

I adopt this course the more decidedly from the conviction that, whatever may be the uncertain boundary-line of Your Excellency's office, and whether this is found to be a question lying within or without that line, that, at all events, it must not only enlist in my cause all the equitable dispositions of your mind, but, for one over-ruling reason, must secure me the whole official aid which it is in Your Excellency's power to bestow. That reason is, that Your Excellency's neutrality would be fatal to me. Should my apprehensions prove just, and a disposition to violate my agreement with the Emperor actually manifest itself, how utterly futile would be the hope that the French Ministry would heed me, when my own Government withdrew from me both its countenance and coöperation.

My "Memorial," (which is still in the custody of the Minister of the Marine,) was submitted merely as the basis of a Treaty, and not as a final dismissal of the subject from my hands; and I feel it to be a serious grievance that, almost immediately upon the receipt of that document, the French Government should have ceased its communications with me. I feel this the more, from the fact that the Memorial in question was never intended for its present destination. It was a mere impromptu, written in Washington shortly after the library of Congress had been burnt, and at a time when that city contained but few authorities necessary to the elucidation of the subject. I could, therefore, if permitted, have given a much greater fulness of demonstration to its details, and could even have pointed out the very Bureau of His Majesty's Government, upon whose shelves had reposed, for over one hundred years, some of the most convincing evidence the subject admits of.

I am justified, therefore, in the assumption, brief as was the array of facts contained in my Memorial, that, from the silence of the French Government, they were esteemed sufficient for the determination of the entire subject, and that, without further appeal of any kind to me, the Government felt that it already had access to all the intelligence it could desire.

From present impressions, the only aid Your Excellency could render me, would be to secure for me another and an

early audience of the Emperor,—for, whatever direction things may take, His Majesty's honor and magnanimity are, after all, my principal resource.
I have the honor to be,
With great consideration and respect,
Your Excellency's obedient servant,
R. A. PARRISH, Jr.
To His Excellency, J. Y. Mason, Minister Plenipotentiary, &c., &c., Paris.

1854, June 8.—The Claimant wrote to the Emperor, and received his reply through the Grand Chamberlain 19th June, as follows:

From Mr. Parrish to the Emperor. [*No.* 1.]

PARIS, June 8, 1854.

SIRE:—In the month of October last Your Majesty conferred upon me the distinguished honor of an audience, for the purpose of hearing a Proposition to which I had invited the attention of your Government, relatively "to the extension of the French flag over the gold regions of Africa." This Proposition having received your Imperial approbation, I was referred to His Excellency, the Minister of the Marine, with the understanding that he would receive Your Majesty's orders to consider my demonstrations, and, if they were such as to warrant the serious action of the government, that he should enter with me into a Treaty, securing to me the conditions which Your Majesty's munificence had propounded. Accordingly on the first day of November, I submitted to His Excellency such proofs as I deemed sufficient to establish the theoretical value of the case, and more than was adequate to furnish a basis for the Treaty. As early as the third day of December, (as I am constrained to infer from a series of Imperial decrees commencing then,) His Excellency had already decided favorably upon my Proposition, and had determined to carry it into execution. His Excellency's satisfaction with my proofs was the more plainly expressed from the fact that he solicited no further light on the subject than that which was embodied in the documents first received from me. Notwithstanding this, the Treaty has not yet been given to me. My own action was taken through an unshaken confidence in Your Majesty's august Parole; and I am sure Your Majesty remains ignorant of the long suspense in which I am held. It is my urgent duty to return to the United States at the close of the coming week, and I venture, therefore, to solicit a further audience of Your Majesty, as well in consideration of my

Maison
DE L'EMPEREUR

Cabinet
DU
GRAND CHAMBELLAN

Palais de Saint-Cloud le 19 Juin 1854

Monsieur,

J'ai l'honneur de vous prévenir que l'Empereur ne peut vous recevoir, en ce moment en audience particulière, comme vous en avez témoigné le désir.

Agréez, Monsieur, l'assurance de ma considération très distinguée,

Le grand Chambellan,
Duc de Bassano

Monsieur Robert Parish

personal interests as of those of Your Majesty's Government in its relations with this subject.

I have the honor to be, with great respect, Your Majesty's obedient servant.

R. A. PARRISH, JR.,
No. 6 au Rond Point Champs Elysées.

Reply of the Emperor.

PALAIS DE ST. CLOUD, le 19 Juin, 1854.

Maison de l'Empereur,
Cabinet du Grand Chambellin,
Monsieur:

J' ai l' honneur de vous prevenir que l' Empereur ne peut vous recevoir en ce moment, en audience particulière comme vous en avez temoigné le desir.

Agrèez Monsieur, l' assurance de ma consideration tres distinguée,
Le Grand Chambellin,
Monsieur ROBERT PARRISH. DUC DE BASSANO.

Translation.

PALACE OF ST. CLOUD, June 19, 1854.

Residence of the Emperor,
Office of the Grand Chamberlain.

SIR:—I have the honor to apprise you that the Emperor cannot receive you, *just now*, in private audience *pursuant to your expressed desire.*

Receive, Sir, the assurance of my very distinguished consideration.

The Grand Chamberlain,
MR. ROBERT PARRISH. DUKE OF BASSANO.

From Mr. Fould, Minister of State, to Mr. Parrish. [*No. 2.*]

PARIS, le 27 Juin, 1854.

Ministère d'Etat,
Secretariat Général,
Bureau du Secretariat.

Il n'y a pas lieu de donner suite aux propositions de MM. R. Parrish et son Associé tendant à l'exploitation des richesses aurifères de la Senegambie.

Il résulte Monsieur des communicationes qui m'ont eté faites par mon collegue Mr. le Ministre de la Marine et des Colonies, que les Territoires, auxquels se rapportent vos propositions tendant à l'exploitation des gites aurifères de la Senegambie, appartiennent à la France, et que dès lors, il n'y a pas lieu, de donner suite à ces propositions.

Recevez, Monsieur, l'assurance
de ma parfaite considération,
le Ministre d'Etat,
ACHILLE FOULD.

A Monsieur PARRISH,
6 Rond Point des Champs Elysées.

TRANSLATION.

From the Minister of State to Mr. Parrish.

PARIS, June 27, 1854.

Ministry of State,
General Secretaryship,
Office of the Secretaryship.

There is no occasion to pursue the subject submitted by Messrs. Parrish and his Partner, relating to the working of the gold mines of Senegambia.

It results, sir, from the communications addressed to me by my colleague, the Minister of the Marine and the Colonies, that the regions to which your Propositions respecting the working of gold mines in Senegambia refer, belong to France, and that, accordingly, there is no occasion to pursue the matter further.

Receive, Sir, the assurance of my perfect consideration,
The Minister of State,
ACHILLE FOULD.

To Mr. PARRISH,
No. 6 au Rond Point des Champs Elysées.

When, in October, 1853, the foregoing Memorial was delivered to the Emperor, the French colony of Senegal was defined by various writers and by the official reports of the French Government, in the manner following:

"Colony of Senegal.—A name derived from the Senegal river, and given to *some small French colonial* settlements on the West Coast of Africa, comprising several islands and a *small portion* of the African continent between the Senegal and Gambia rivers."—McCulloch's Univ. Gaz., N. Y. 8vo, 1848, Vol. II, p. 793.

Ministère d'État.

Secrétariat général

Bureau du Secrétariat

Paris le 2 Juin 1854

Il n'y a pas lieu de donner suite une proposition de M.M. R. Parish en son associé, tendant à l'exploitation des richesses aurifères de la Sénégambie.

Il résulte, Monsieur, des communications qui m'ont été faites par mon collègue, M. le Ministre de la Marine et des Colonies, que les territoires auxquels se rapportent vos propositions tendant à l'exploitation des gîtes aurifères de la Sénégambie, appartiennent à la France et que, dès lors, il n'y a pas lieu de donner suite à ces propositions.

Recevez, Monsieur, l'assurance de ma parfaite considération

Le Ministre d'État

À Monsieur Parish, 6. Rond-Point des Champs Élysées.

"Senegal.—A French Colony in Africa.—It is composed of several islands and *a part of* Senegambia, situated *at the mouth of the River Senegal*."—Dic. Univ., Perrot & Co., Paris 4to, 1843, Vol. II, p. 416.

The same definition of the colony will also be found in Malte Brun's Geography, Paris, 8vo, 1841, Vol. V, p. 609, and in all the standard works on Geography up to 1853, as well as in the Preface to the City Directory of Paris of that year, as published by M. Fould himself, &c., &c., &c., and also in all official documents of France.

The petty commerce of this colony with the tribes on the River Senegal was, at that date, a privilege only enjoyed and purchased by France by means of *annual contributions* paid to the native kings (as will presently be shown); a circumstance which demonstrates the very feeble limits, power, and pretensions of the colony. But an immense change immediately ensued, not only in the condition and character of the colony itself, and even in that of Senegambia also, but throughout the whole of that vast area of the African continent lying north of the Equator, and particularized in the Memorial. In Prof. Blackie's Imperial Gazetteer, London, 8vo, 1855, (only two years later,) is the following: "Senegambia— An extensive region of West Africa, lying between the Senegal and Gambia. Such at least would be its extension if the application of the name were determined by its derivation. But the name of Senegambia has been brought into use *chiefly by French writers,* who affecting to have extensive national claims to territory in West Africa, *have gone on enlarging continually the application of the name,* (which is more properly given to their own settlements,) and understand by Senegambia the whole country from the Senegal south to the Sierra Leone, Cape St. Ann, *or even to Cape Palmas!* Such nomenclature, however, founded neither on physical features, nor on political divisions, serves no useful purpose."—Vol. II, pp. 884, 886. [The author should have added—unless vast changes had been initiated in Africa prior to the date of Mr. Fould's letter to the Claimant, of 27 June, 1854, given above.]

In vindication of the Claimant's reply to that letter, the following quotation from the same Gazetteer may be thought pertinent. Art. Gambia.—"A British colony, and river of West Africa. The former *occupies both banks of the latter*, including some of its islands, &c., &c., Besides the settlements above mentioned, there are *numerous factories and stations at intervals along both banks* of the stream."—Vol. I, p. 1054.

Coupling with these indisputable truths the hardy asseverations of the letter in question of Mr. Fould, it will inspire amazement that the Prime Minister of the French Empire, from motives so manifestly sordid and ignoble, could have so far falsified the palpable truth.

Mr. Parrish to the Minister of the French Marine. [*No.* 3.]

LE HAVRE, 4 July, 1854.

SIR:—My letter (No. 2) to Your Excellency, of the sixth of June, remains still unanswered. Finding myself now abruptly recalled to America, I cannot hope for a reply to it until some few weeks hence, on my return to France.

I was on the 27th ultimo, however, honored by a letter from His Excellency, the Minister of State, Mr. Fould, whose contents are of a character so truly incomprehensible that I have conceived it proper, before my departure, to apprise Your Excellency of the fact, and combat the erroneous positions it assumes.

His Excellency is pleased to allude to a Proposition alleged to have been submitted by myself and an Associé for the working of gold mines situated in Senegambia! He then proceeds to say that Senegambia belongs to the French, and that, accordingly, there is no occasion to pursue the subject further! He quotes Your Excellency, moreover, as his authority for these assertions. I can but imperfectly express my amazement that the facts of the case should have suffered at His Excellency's hands such an extraordinary perversion. His letter, overflowing with error, is scarcely in any one particular in harmony with the facts.

I. He alleges that I have an Associé.
II. That my proposition refers to the *working of mines*.
III. That the scene of this proposition is *Senegambia*.

I beg leave, respectfully, but most emphatically, to rebut all these allegations.

I. The Proposition submitted by me was purely my own; originated with myself and was offered in my own name; and, indeed, His Excellency was personally aware that, in my correspondence, or conversation either, with His Majesty, Your Excellency, or with himself, I had not at any time alluded to the existence of an Associé. I had a pecuniary engagement with one person prior to leaving America, but this was sundered long ago, and has never been mentioned in connection with the subject. Mr. ———, it is true, introduced me to His Excellency, but not in the capacity of my Associé; nor can I suppose he can have so far forgotten himself as to have ventured, without authority, upon the assumption of such a relation toward me. He was most urgent to be named as a party in the Traité, and to receive from me a power of attorney to represent me whilst I was in Italy; but neither of these petitions was acceded to. On the contrary, I merely promised to pay him liberally for his services (upon terms proposed by himself), but dreamed not of confiding an interest of so much weight to such weak and incapable hands. His horrible falsehoods, since, have discharged me both in morals and in law from every obligation toward him, and have amply vindicated the wisdom of my having excluded him, at the beginning, from all trust, confidence or responsibility. When, therefore, His Excellency speaks of an Associé as being identified with me in any papers, I can only suppose that he alludes to papers which I have never seen, and of the contents of which I disclaim all knowledge.

II. In the second place, His Excellency speaks of a Proposition for the actual working of gold mines. If by this it is meant to allege that my Proposition embodied an application for mining privileges, I deny the assertion as utterly groundless and untrue. If it be the purpose of the French Government to embark in the working of the mines as a party interested, as I assume to be the case from the contents of your own and His Excellency's letters, as well as from the express language of His Majesty to me, I have nothing to object. But I do strenuously object (if such a thing be meant,) to the allegation that I have been an applicant for mining privileges. My Proposition was political and diplomatic, not mechanical. It was to extend the eagle of the Empire for a thousand miles beyond its present limits, over regions whose opulence is unparalleled upon the face of the globe, whose agricultural wealth alone outstrips the riches of the Indies, whilst their wealth in gold, as I have only too plainly demonstrated, almost transcends the possibility of belief. These scenes, whose history I had minutely conned, and whose geological resources were probably more familiar to myself than any other person, were for all practical purposes literally unknown. Abandoned to savages as an irreclaimable wilderness, it has been the habit of scholars of all nations to regard them as bearing an impracticable relation to any enlarged scheme for the prosperity, civilization or happiness of mankind. I, for the first time, materialized this knowledge, and gave to it an immense and an immediate practical value. But so far from my having proposed such a thing as to *work these mines*, it was from His Majesty's own lips that this proposal originally proceeded. His own suggestion was, that the Government of France should work them, and divide their produce equally with me for a number of years. But this proposal, however flattering and munificent, I have already declined. In like manner, when His Majesty demanded "if I would accompany the Expedition," I replied "that I would not go from choice, but, if it were thought necessary, would do so." Such a reply is scarcely reconcilable with the idea of an application for mining privileges.

III. In the third place, His Excellency takes the extraordinary ground that the Kong Mountains are in Senegambia, and that Senegambia belongs to the French. These allegations are advanced *upon Your Excellency's authority*, and are adduced as reasons (in the midst of an active colonial campaign) why my scheme should not be prosecuted. These are grave mistakes. It is rather invidious to be supposed to school His Excellency upon the geography of the Empire, but I must be allowed to demonstrate his deficient intelligence in both these particulars. The Kong Mountains are not in Senegambia, and Senegambia does not belong to the French. If Senegambia now appertains to the Empire, it has been acquired both by conquest and diplomacy since the first day of November, 1853, in pursuance of my own directions, and accordingly does not weaken my claims upon the Government of France. At that date there was one, and I believe two English posts on the right bank of the Gambia above Pisania. The title of the French was very vague even to a portion of this vast region, as, indeed, the recent conquests of Pohdor and Djalmath incontestably avouch. But these conquests and the present extension of her authority over the whole of Senegambia (even if this point be admitted to be true) are the most cogent reasons that could be advanced (if France were anxious to be thought just to me) for observing her engagements toward me with religious fidelity. Such an acquisition is the immediate and logical fruit of the intelligence I have imparted to her, and the simple reason why her dominion over Senegambia has been heretofore a mere theory instead of a fact, is because, until I enlightened her as to its value, she very properly attached but a trivial importance to it. That value, however, is not as His Excellency seems to surmise, because of the gold which it contains. Senegambia contains no gold. It is merely valuable as the highway to the auriferous regions which lie beyond. The area specified in my Memorial was the region traversed by the Kong Mountains, commencing in *Nigritia*, in the Kingdom of Bambouk, just beyond the confines of Senegambia, and extending for the distance of a thousand miles south-eastward to the banks of the Quorra. Senegambia, according to the best geographers, does not extend into Nigritia. It comprises the alluvial plains between the Gambia and the Senegal, reaching no further from the coast than the swamp of Dendoudé Tiali, a swamp whose waters' during the rainy season uniting the Gambia with the Falèmé, convert the whole of Senegambia into a temporary island. The French flag has never been displayed within the boundaries of Bambouk. A hundred years ago there were French trading posts as far as Galam (both at St. Joseph's on the Senegal and at St. Pierre's on the Falèmé), but these were remote from Bambouk, nor can they be assumed to lend any support on the part of France to the pretence either of past or present authority over that kingdom. Instead of the exercise of authority, the fate of these Forts looks much more like an inability either to acquire or to maintain it. It is, indeed, an exhibition of remarkable fatuity on the part of the Government of that day, that for such barren results as the mere ordinary commerce of the river, they should have toiled up almost within sight of this alluring land, and with published accounts of its riches in their possession, should have abandoned its pursuit, and turning away, even permitted their adjacent fortifications to sink into decay. In short, the allusions of the Minister of State to the geography of this quarter of Africa are so exceedingly inexact, and evince so imperfect a knowledge of the limits of the Empire, that relatively to my Proposition I esteem them to be destitute of meaning. I am convinced, therefore, that there is a misunderstanding, and that Your Excellency never could have lent your authority to opinions so singularly destitute of all foundation. Indeed, Your Excellency must very well remember (on the occasion when my Memorial was given into your hands) we examined your maps together, and whilst I pointed out the region to which I referred, Your Excellency admitted to me that St. Joseph's and St. Pierre's (still marked on the map) were the ultima thule of the French dominions. Your Excellency did not insinuate that then, or ever before, there had been a French post within the Kingdom of Bambouk. Nay, more than this, when I saw Your Excellency for the second time, on the fifth of December, 1853, so plainly did you corroborate these previous impressions, as to tell me that you were then organizing an Expedition, which, as the event has shown, was for the conquest of this identical region, and also told me in answer to my inquiry to that effect, that you thought you could venture to say "that I would not be urged to accompany the Expedition," as His Majesty had in a measure requested. What, then, am I to infer from the discrepancy between this language to me, and that of your communications, as above quoted, from the Minister of State? Surely the Minister of State would not have me believe that France was about to conquer a colony *already in her possession,* or that it has taken him nine months, with all the aid of Your Excellency's advice, to be able to define the boundary of the Empire!

But it is superfluous to dwell at greater length upon his conspicuous errors, for as Your Excellency in candor will at once admit, they are quite irrelevant to the issue between us. His Majesty has placed me in communication with you, and it remains for Your Excellency, as early as your other duties will allow, to send me, on my return to France, a copy of the Traité.

I have the honor to be with distinguished consideration,
   Your Excellency's Obedient Servant,
        R. A. PARRISH, Jr.
To His Excellency, M. Theodore Ducos,
 Ministre de la Marine, &c., &c., à Paris.

1854, July 4.—The Claimant's letters and remittances being still stopped in the Post-offices, he was obliged to return to America.

*   *   *   *   *   *   *   *   *

1856, Sept. 20.—The Claimant returned to France and wrote to Admiral Hamelin, (successor to Mr. Ducos, deceased,) Paris, 3d Oct., 1856, enclosing a letter to the Emperor, and giving the evidence of the payment, by England, of two hundred thousand dollars, or its equivalent, to Mr. Hargreaves, for demonstrating the gold fields of Australia, after a distinct refusal to make any engagement with him in advance. It elicited no notice. Another letter to the Admiral, of 15th Oct , 1856, complaining that the trunks and papers of the Claimant were habitually rifled, likewise elicited no notice, viz :

Mr. Parrish to the Minister of the Marine, [*No.* 4,] *enclosing his Letter to the Emperor,* [*No.* 2.]

         Paris, 3d Oct., 1856.

Sir:—Will Your Excellency deign to do me the distinguished favor of laying the enclosed letter, with the accompanying Book and Correspondence, at the earliest practical moment, before the Emperor?

With sentiments of perfect consideration I am Your Excellency's obedient servant.
        R. A. PARRISH, Jr.,
        Hotel Meurice, Rue de Rivoli.
To His Excellency, Admiral Hamelin,
 Minister of State, &c., &c., Paris.

Claimant's Letter to the Emperor. [*No.* 2.]

PARIS, 3 October, 1856.

SIRE:—Some three years ago I was honored by Your Majesty with an Extraordinary Audience, in order to submit a Proposition which it was conceded on all sides would make an important epoch in the financial history of France. The rich fruits of that Proposition France is now enjoying. However obvious may have seemed its truths, on a perusal of a part only of my demonstrations, the prodigious scope of the enterprise itself, and the voluminous evidence by which it was sustained, were only made conclusive, nevertheless, after prolonged and arduous research on my part, achieved under circumstances of peculiar discouragement. It embodied, moreover, a purely original idea, known only to myself, and revealed alone, *under the inviolable sanctity of Your Majesty's parole.* That parole, too—as an indispensable pre-requisite to its surrender—was exacted by reasons of unusual force. Not only was the subject confidential in its nature to an eminent degree—to whose value even an unguarded whisper might have been fatal—and whose disclosure (as I have elsewhere said) I was once compelled to prevent at the hazard of my life, but from the well understood composition of all Ministries could not wisely have been entrusted to their diplomatic and irresponsible honor. If this were generally true in principle, it was additionally true in France, the entire authority of whose Government (then in a transition state) was centred in Your Majesty. To my mind, it was irrefutable, that a community which contained a standing army of four hundred thousand men had ceased to act and reason for itself, and that Your Majesty's voice, therefore, was the only law of France. To Your Majesty alone I looked, and still look, both for the appreciation and remuneration of my scheme.

Since its surrender, under Your Majesty's directions, to His Excellency, the Minister of the Marine, a hint reached me, bearing the authority of His Excellency, the Minister of State, that something (relatively to the execution of the Traité) was to be apprehended on the score of ridicule. The meaning of this hint was not expounded to me, nor am I able to comprehend it. It certainly has no equitable application here, nor indeed in any case involving the development of a great new idea; least of all, when pregnant with such magnificent results. Nor did the First Consul think so: "The power of the French Republic should henceforth consist in this, that not a single new idea should exist which is not indebted for its birth to its exertions." Such was the expression of his truly Imperial mind! But suppose, Sire, that in addressing myself first to some other Government this tremendous prize, thus lying for ages before the very eyes of France, had been seized by them! In such a case his Excellency's hint would have become perfectly intelligible. To have escaped from so fatal a disaster France can well afford to pay me fifteen millions of francs, or even thrice fifteen That this disaster would have happened, but for Your Majesty's promises to me, is absolutely certain. I have in my possession proofs to that effect, of a character altogether convincing, which I beg permission to lay before Your Majesty, evincing that I can elsewhere now obtain many millions of francs for the same Proposition.

It is utterly inconceivable that Your Majesty, born a Prince, bred a gentleman, and elevated by your great office so far beyond the reach of every vulgar motive, could feel the least inclination to violate either my personal rights or any great principle of justice. I therefore urge that this point should be gravely pondered by Your Majesty, and that I should be placed in *statu quo ante negotiationem*, or be put in receipt of that plain alternative which Your Majesty's promise has guaranteed.

Golberry, who wrote and reasoned better of Bambouk than any one either before or since, observes [chap. xiii] that the annual value of its gold (together with all the other commerce of the Kingdom) might be made to amount to five hundred thousand francs; but from the extreme uncertainty and difficulty attending its conquest dissuaded his Government [ch. xi] from making the attempt. His whole thought in fact was of commerce—nothing else. Like the whole human race he was "serenely" blind to the true geological wealth of the African continent. I have written and I am sure also that I have studied and traveled more in this connection than Golberry himself.

Rey, Raffenel, Huard, Hecquard, and the entire catalogue of travelers, who during the present century have either visited or written of Bambouk, have told us less, much less than Golberry. But neither they nor he so much as dreamed of the infinite mineral value of this region. Rey, for example, says, "Il est vrai qu' on pourrait en peu de temps appauvrir la mine," [Rev. Col., Jan., 1854, p. 53,] little surmising that he was speaking of a vast auriferous deposit, surmounting in value the aggregated wealth of nations, and as inexhaustible as time itself! In fact, none of them beheld there objects of real national importance, nor did they by their revelations exercise the most trivial influence over the policy of France. They had all, before my arrival, been incorporated into the columns of the Moniteur, and for the most part under the immediate supervision of His Excellency, M. Fould: a circumstance affording the most triumphant vindication of the originality of my Proposition which it is possible to conceive. On this point it closes all argument.

Looking to the example of England in a similar case, I cannot but feel aggrieved when I remember the delays and even the indignities, Sire, to which I have been subjected, and of the details of which I am sure Your Majesty is insufficiently advised. My very unprofitable correspondence with Your Majesty's Ministers, comprising six letters (copies of which are sent herewith), will afford perhaps some partial explanation. The North British Review for August, 1854, (also sent) demonstrates that after the Australian gold fields had been discovered and proclaimed by the most renowned geologists living, (not only by their reports to learned societies, and by published books, and by appeals to the English public through the newspapers, but also even by letters urgently addressed to the Colonial and Home Governments,) and even after reiterated offers to make the disclosure for small sums of money had been *distinctly refused*, whereby all pretence of subsequent discovery was annihilated, that still, in the face of all this, upon their ultimate disclosure by a traveler from California, eight or ten years later, he was made the recipient of gratuities amounting, or equivalent to a million of francs! Such is the value attached by nations to these gigantic acquisitions, *even when the wealth is on their own soil*, and when no promises of reward have been the motives and the reasons for its realization! To this volume Your Majesty's attentive heed is invited; for it displays also, in a remarkable light, the sturdy blindness and obtuseness of Governments on these subjects, to which rule Your Majesty presents but an individual exception.

Since the receipt of my documents by His Excellency, the late M. Ducos, partly owing to the illness and death of a brother (who required my personal cares), and partly to other reasons, I have been enabled to pass but a limited time in France, and to this, possibly, amongst many causes (with whose detail I would not willingly fatigue Your Majesty), the little progress my interests have made may be ascribed. It may be appropriate here to observe, however, that no one, at any time, has had authority to write, to act, or to speak for me in the premises, saving one person only, who (in the capacity of messenger, and *with no other power*,) was deputed to deliver a certain message and to arrange the hour of my interviews with Your Majesty's Ministers.

The éclat, which from its stupendous proportions, may justly attach to this subject, I value not. I have other and more congenial objects of ambition. I seek from the fulfillment of Your Majesty's Parole but to confer on my father and his family the ample means of happiness. I will propose, therefore, a compromise, if Your Majesty will indulge me with a further audience, which will divest this point of difficulty, and, if desired will bury my whole connection with the subject in permanent oblivion. I have already made such arrangements that the funds due to me may be remitted to America without occasioning remark.

I have now been delayed for three years from that prosperity which I cannot but consider my legitimate right, and which would have been largely realized upon the mere delivery of the Traité. Three years, Sire, is a long period of suspense to be passed in contemplating an exalted hope, as no human being better knows than Your Majesty. Besides, we are all of us going rapidly to our graves. Some of the leading actors in this enterprise are already there. If, therefore, Your Majesty's munificent promises are ever to benefit either me or mine, I earnestly entreat their undelayed fulfillment. This all-absorbing theme has now consumed eight years of my life; has brought me to the brink of bankruptcy, and has at length become an insupportable burthen to my time, my resources, and even to my happiness.

Weary with delay, I remain, Sire,
Of Your Majesty the obedient servant,
R. A. PARRISH, Jr.
To His Majesty the Emperor.

Mr. Parrish to His Ex'y the Minister of the French Marine. [*No.* 5.]

PARIS, 15 October, 1856.

SIR:—I deem it proper to acquaint Your Excellency with the fact, that my trunk has recently been opened, and its contents subjected to examination. It contained, together with many papers, a book, shutting with a lock, in which were memoranda, bearing an important relation to the subject of my late letter to His Majesty. A much-prized map, executed by myself, appears to have been purloined.

The circumstances attending this infamy convince me that the locks of my trunk and book must have been picked in reiterated instances.

These occurrences transpired at my apartment, No. 20 Rue D'Antin; the key of which, during my absence, was invariably entrusted to M. De la Pierre, who is at once the proprietor and concierge of the house.

I have the honor to be, with sentiments of distinguished consideration, Your Excellency's obedient servant.
ROBERT A. PARRISH, Jr.,
Hotel Meurice, Rue de Rivoli.
To His Excellency, ADMIRAL HAMELIN,
Minister of State for the Marine and Colonies,
&c., &c., &c., Paris.

In the autumn of 1856, soon after the Claimant's arrival in

Paris, he called on His Excellency, Mr. August Belmont, U. S. Minister to Holland, then on a visit to Paris, to solicit his intervention with Mr. Mason, to accomplish a settlement of this Claim. The Claimant's correspondence with the French Government was exhibited to him, whereupon he kindly consented to see what could be done.

A few days afterwards he reported that he found he could do nothing.

When, in 1860, an affidavit of these facts was written for to Mr. Belmont, the affidavit was *anonymously* returned, accompanied by a memorandum that "*he had no knowledge of the Claim!*"

A little later, when the Claimant called on him to excuse the trouble, if any, occasioned by this appeal to him, Mr. Belmont responded in the sense of the "anonymous" memorandum, but with a very angry and emphatic manner; thereby evincing that for some unexplained reason the subject seemed to be *an irritating one*. It is certain, however, that his knowledge of the claim equaled, if it did not exceed that of the Claimant himself, whatever may have been his reasons for suppressing it.

On his way to France the Claimant had recently passed through Holland and Belgium, with both of which governments, and subsequently with Prussia, he opened a negotiation of a like nature with that with France, in the consummation of which he was frustrated by the emissaries of Mr. Fould; but he is thus enabled to prove that neither of those governments deemed from six to ten millions of francs too high a price for such a vast national benefit as he has conferred on France.

Affidavit of S. L. Gouverneur, Esq., late U. S. Consul to Foo Chow.

Samuel L. Gouverneur, being duly sworn according to law, deposes and says: That some time in the year 1850, this deponent became acquainted, in Washington, D. C., with Robert A. Parrish, Jr.; that about the close of 1852 or spring of 1853, the said R. A. Parrish, Jr., then in Washington, communicated to this deponent that he had a Proposition to offer to the Government of the United States, by which they might acquire a territory as valuable in mineral wealth and commercial importance as California or Australia; that this territory was so situated that it could be taken possession of without fear of molestation or interference by any of the other Powers of the world. Upon inquiry, he informed this deponent that said territory was not on the American continent, whereupon this deponent stated emphatically that no effort could be made by the United States Government to avail itself of his discovery, from constitutional objections. Subsequently the said Parrish told this deponent that he intended to offer his Proposition to the Government of France.

This deponent subsequently, in the summer of 1854, again met the said Parrish at Willard's Hotel in Washington, who told him that he had been to France, had had a special and extraordinary audience of the Emperor of the French, and had submitted his plans and Proposition to the French Government, on the pledge of the Emperor that if the French took possession of the designated territory in Africa, that he, the said Parrish, should receive the sum of fifteen millions of francs. The said Parrish then and there told this deponent the particulars of the said audience with the Emperor, what the Emperor said, &c., &c. This deponent, from the immensity of the sum, had at first entertained almost a feeling of incredulity upon the subject, but the said Parrish then and there showed him certain official letters and papers, as well as copies of the Paris Moniteur, by which this deponent was convinced that not only had an Expedition sailed from France for the designated territory, and that the said Parrish's Proposition had also seriously engaged the attention of the French Government, but that they had already taken advantage of it. The said Parrish then and there also told this deponent that he had been treated by the French Ministry with duplicity and unfairness, but that if he could only see the Emperor again, he believed justice would be done him, but that outside parties in France were reaping, he feared, the rewards of his industry and study unknown to the Emperor. The said Parrish then mentioned to this deponent that he had not confided all the knowledge he had to the French Government in relation to the auriferous regions in Africa, and this deponent, at the instance of the said Parrish, submitted a Proposition to the Prussian Government, through Baron Grabow, (Secretary of Legation to Baron Gerolt, Prussian Minister,) for the sum of six millions of francs, to put the Government of Prussia in possession of an auriferous territory similar in value to that which he had offered to France. The Proposition was seriously considered by the Government of Prussia, without objection to the sum mentioned, and this deponent received a letter from the said Baron Grabow declining the Proposition on other grounds

In or about the month of April, A. D., eighteen hundred and

sixty, this deponent accompanied said Parrish to the United States Department of State at Washington, with a view to ascertain how the written synopsis of the claim of said Parrish on the French Government, filed by him in writing, as "a claim based upon the personal Parole of the Emperor," had been altered and erroneously printed in the list of claims furnished to the United States Senate by that Department. Judge Hogan, who had charge of the French Claims, replied to said Parrish's inquiries that he, the Judge, had made the alteration under an impression that it would be to the interest and advantage of Mr. Parrish that it should be so altered. In conclusion, this deponent further states, that at one time in Washington, in the spring of 1853, the said Parrish had serious difficulties with parties that he had taken into his confidence in the premises, and as it seemed with good reason at the time, to this deponent, expected a personal attack upon him. This deponent further says that he has no interest in the claim aforesaid.

[STAMP.]   SAM. L. GOUVERNEUR.

Sworn and subscribed before me, this 8th day of April, 1867.
LEWIS GODBOU, Alderman.

1856, Nov. and Dec.—The Claimant registered his name repeatedly during these two months for an audience of the Emperor, in the Reception Book at the Tuileries kept there for that purpose, but in vain.

Mr. Parrish to His Excellency, Mr. Mason. [No. 2.]

PARIS, 24 Sept., 1856.

SIR:—When I had the honor of waiting upon Your Excellency a few days ago you were in London, and your absence indefinite. I avail myself of this method, therefore, of requesting that you will have the great goodness of placing me on your next list of presentations to His Majesty. I shall remain in Paris some time.

This, as I understand, is a courtesy uniformily extended to Bearers of Dispatches at all the Courts of Europe.

I have the honor to be, with distinguished consideration, Your Excellency's obedient servant,
R. A. PARRISH, Jr.
To His Excellency, Hon. J. Y. MASON,   Bearer of Dis.
Ambassador, &c.

Official Note of Mr. Parrish's Presentation at Court.

PARIS, LE 26 Dec., 1856.
Legation des Etats Unis, MR. PARRISH.

SIR:—The Minister of the United States is informed that he

will have the honor to present you to their Majesties on Sunday next, 28th inst, at the Tuileries. Mr. Mason will be obliged if you will be at his house 13 Rue Beaujon on that day, at 12¼ o'clock, prepared to accompany him to the Palace.

Very respectfully,

In uniform. I. B. WILBUR, Secretary.

Second and Public Audience of the Claimant by the EMPEROR.

1856, Dec. 28.—The Claimant was presented by the Ambassador of the United States to their Majesties, at a public audience at the Tuileries, when he informed the Emperor that his interests in connection with his African proposition had been involved in a difficulty by His Excellency, Mr. Fould, from which he could not extricate himself without the Emperor's aid, and requested another private audience with a view to an arrangement. The Emperor said he should certainly have a private audience, and inquired how long he would remain in Paris. He replied that he had no other business in France but this, and as soon as it was settled he would leave. The Emperor then repeated that he should have another audience. But no action was ever taken on these promises.

Immediately thereafter the Claimant was the victim of renewed and formidable persecutions intended to expel him, and whose effect was to expel him from Paris before said private audience could be accomplished. Lewd women, authorized by Mr. Fould, assumed possession of the key of the Claimant's domicile and intruded therein against his wishes and protestations both by night and by day; his letters and drafts from America were again totally intercepted and stopped in the French Post-office; his trunks, books and papers were habitually and insolently explored by spies; he was absolutely quarantined from all visitors by their being systematically told he was "not at home," even whilst he was awaiting them by appointment, whereby both his business and his social intercourse with the community were absolutely cut off; a hired spy (one Dentist, of Philadelphia,) was employed and instigated, amongst other things, to betray the Claimant's American correspondence to the French police, and also pertinaciously, although vainly, to insist on leaving at his lodgings an enormous knife (suitable only for an assassin), whereby the most odious reflections upon him might be supported; slanders, moreover, of the vilest kind were industriously disseminated against him amongst the Americans in Paris, with a view to alienate from him their respect and sympathy; (amongst the rest that he had been arrested and imprisoned for gross misconduct,) and multifarious intrigues, unfamiliar to the experience and genius of the American people, were set on foot with unexampled industry and audacity to destroy at once his character and his life.

Letter of His Excellency H. M. Watts, late U. S. Minister to Austria, to Mr. Parrish.

PHILADELPHIA, Walnut St., 29th April, 1859.

MY DEAR SIR:—I remember your presentation by our Minister, Mr. Mason, to the Emperor of the French, in December, 1856. I have not retained a memorandum of the date, but believe it to have been, as stated in your note of the 22d inst., to which this is a reply.

Mrs. Watts and myself were received at the same time by both the Emperor and Empress in the Palais des Tuileries. The number of persons introduced by Mr. Mason, on that occasion, it was said, was unusually large, and our detention at his hotel where we met was so long that many of our carriages did not arrive at the palace at the moment appointed for the reception; in consequence thereof, some who were in the advance were received, while many of us in the rear were waiting in an adjoining hall to know the pleasure of the Emperor. During this suspense some apprehension was felt and expressed, that, as we had failed in punctuality, the etiquette of the Court would necessarily exclude us. You thought we would not be received for a different reason, one entirely personal, and spoke quite indignantly about it.

Your reason was that one or more of the Ministers of the Emperor designed to prevent your personal interview with His Majesty. When the Emperor and Empress therefore entered the salon where we were, and proceeded along the line formed for our introduction, I particularly observed your presentation to him, and thought that your conversation, which is generally mere ceremony, was continued longer than usual. Being far from you, I did not hear a word of it.

I have the honor to be, very respectfully, yours, &c.

H. M. WATTS.

R. A. PARRISH, Fourth and Walnut Sts. Phila.

P. S.—Soon after the event as above-mentioned there was a rumor in Paris of your arrest. H. M. WATTS.

The tardy arrival of part of the Imperial guests on this occasion was the result of a trick. The Claimant was assigned by Mr. Mason to a position near the rear of the line of carriages. As the line was crossing the court yard of the Tuileries, it was intersected in the middle by the cortège of the Prince Imperial, (then an infant) which was just setting out to give him an airing. The delay thus occasioned was much greater than necessary, only two four-horse chariots and a troop of horse having to pass. They purposely moved slowly, however, and detained it as many minutes as they could, prolonging the time by some halting. This, under the strict ceremonial of such occasions, could never have occurred without the connivance and commands both of the Grand Chamberlain and of the Military Commander of the Palace. It was manifestly preconcerted; as was indeed the whole exceptional character of this day's presentation, lest the unguarded murmurs of the Claimant might arouse any censorious reflections upon the Emperor, from the brilliant assembly.

Those who are unfamiliar with the crafty policy of the French Government, may not at first perceive the motive for these industrious rumors of the Claimant's imprisonment, &c.; but it was a far-seeing one. When a sum of fifteen millions is in question, every official person in France, who can get an interest in it, does so. They accordingly impute the same disposition to others. If, therefore, an attempt were made to defraud, imprison and destroy the Claimant, and powerful statesmen of his own Government were prepared to avenge him, a misstep in that direction would only precipitate a settlement of the claim upon its merits and checkmate the intrigue. It was requisite, therefore, to know *in advance* what friends the Claimant had, and what was the measure of their power. For this purpose, a rumor of his arrest was better than the fact. It inculpated nobody, and yet brought forth an exhibition of his strength. The result proved *that not a human being interfered*. Mr. Mason and Mr. Buchanan had had a conference in London a short time before, and had absolutely *sold the Claimant to the Jews*. No other solution can explain their diabolical misconduct. And when it is perceived that the Empress and the whole Imperial family were capable of the infamy of accepting bribes to ruin him, it is scarcely impossible that the immaculate Mr. Mason, and the still more immaculate and most blessed Buchanan, should do the same thing. That large sums of money were *borrowed* by Mr. Mason from a friend of Mr. Fould (and never repaid) can be readily substantiated. As much as thirteen millions of francs were diffused in bribes in this connection, which is probably the most colossal piece of corruption on record. But it paid. [Vide Mirés' frauds—Post.]

In 1856, the Claimant, at a dinner party, (given by a distinguished Jew banker, and friend of Mr. Fould,) had the amazing honor of being introduced to the Chief of Police of the City of Paris, and also to Colonel Armand, the Hebrew commander of the Imperial Prison of State, at Vincennes! This is the present French Bastile. The Col. was so assiduously polite to the Claimant as gradually to arouse suspicion. An Italian adage says: "If men are more than naturally polite to you, they have either betrayed you, or are going to betray you." Perhaps this dinner itself, and the numerous soirées which followed, were also illustrations of the adage. The Col., on all these occasions, never wearied of descending from the lofty eminence of his high official place to do unceasing honor to the Claimant. Amongst other courtesies, he gave him many and urgent invitations to make a visit to the prison. Strangers often go. The Claimant had already been there prior to his Treaty with the Emperor. One day, after many fruitless verbal invitations, all of which had been cordially accepted, the Colonel visited the Claimant at the Grand Hotel du Louvre, with a special written invitation for him, more gracious in terms, than those accorded to the public. It was to admit him to Vincennes "on any day or hour whatsoever, even in the Colonel's absence!" The Claimant grew thoughtful. The invitation contained no absolute provision for his enlargement in case a draft should slam the door, as he strode through the interior of those historical cells, whose walls are sixteen feet thick. He remembered, that on the demise of the children of Louis Quatorze, rumors arose that the Duke of Orleans (then heir apparent) had practiced upon them; that stung by the insult, he demanded of the Minister of Police a commitment to the Bastile until a trial should establish his innocence. "To the Bastile!"—exclaimed the Minister—"whatever you wish to accomplish, keep out of the Bastile. Let me tell you that a Prince in the Bastile is *utterly powerless.*"

If this were true of a Prince Royal, the Claimant concluded that it was barely possible it might be true of a stranger whose dearest friends were those pitiless, penniless, remorseless rogues, Messieurs Mason and Buchanan. He took advice upon the subject,—the very highest order of advice in Europe. He was counseled to decline the hospitality of Colonel Armand, and to see the Emperor immediately—without a moment's loss of time, or to leave the shores of France forthwith.

A short time afterwards a fearful catastrophe occurred at Vincennes. The stone arched ceiling of one of its cells fell in, (*by accident,*) crushing twenty-eight persons in the ruin. They were either *suspects* or were awaiting trial on various political charges; but were all a *good riddance* to the Government. As soon as they were ascertained to be clearly dead, the French papers pitied them most touchingly.

1857, Jan. 26.—The Claimant wrote again to the Emperor, reminding him of his late promise of another audience, viz:

Mr. Parrish to the Emperor. [*No.* 3.]

Paris, 26 January, 1857,
Au Grand Hotel du Louvre.

Sire:—On the twenty-eighth ultimo, when presented to Your Majesty by the Ambassador of the United States, I received your august and gracious promise of a "private audience," touching my still pending African Proposition. Since its submission to Your Majesty in October, 1853, and notwithstanding the magnificent results into which it has now expanded, my personal interests in connection with it have made no progress. On the contrary, disappointments, delays, and formidable blows struck at me by unseen hands, have thus far been my only recompense; until, at length, after swallowing up all my resources, it threatens to engulf the little that remains to me of hope or happiness. Standing in the centre of angry and most unprincipled intrigues—the inevitable fruit perhaps of the occasion—I experience the pressing and immediate need of Your Majesty's enlightened interposition. This I invoke with the greater confidence, that I have important disclosures still to make, more than equivalent in value to all that has heretofore been promised me. Moreover, if from

CABINET DE L'EMPEREUR.

Palais des Tuileries, le 10 Février 1857

Monsieur,

Occupé exclusivement des affaires particulières de l'Empereur, et me tenant constamment aux Tuileries, auprès de la personne de Sa Majesté, j'ai le regret de ne pouvoir vous assigner un rendez-vous, selon vos désirs. Veuillez, je vous prie, me faire connaître par écrit l'objet dont vous désirez m'entretenir.

Recevez, Monsieur, l'assurance de ma considération distinguée.

Le Secrétaire de l'Empereur
Chef du Cabinet.

Mocquard

W. R. A. Parrish
356 Grand Hôtel du Louvre

reasons of State—of which I am not advised—the execution of the Traité, or the payment of the fifteen millions of francs, should be considered inexpedient, I am willing to suggest modifications of these engagements, to which I am sure Your Majesty would find it easy to accede.

I have the honor to remain, Sire, of Your Majesty the very obedient servant.

R. A. PARRISH, Jr.

To His Majesty, the Emperor.

1857, Feb. 9.—The Claimant wrote to Mr. Mocquard, Private Secretary of the Emperor, soliciting an interview, in order to remind the Emperor, through him, of the lately promised audience.

Mr. Parrish to Mr. Mocquard

PARIS, 9 Feb., 1857.

SIR:—I beg the honor of a momentary interview with you, relative to the letter to His Majesty sent by me some two weeks ago.

I have the honor to remain, with great consideration, your obedient servant.

R. A. PARRISH, Jr.,
Grand Hotel du Louvre.

MR. O. MOCQUARD,
  Chef du Cabinet de L'Empereur,
    No. 216 Rue St. Honoré.

Mr. Mocquard to Mr. Parrish.

PALAIS DES TUILERIES, le 10 Fevrier, 1857.

Cabinet de l'Empereur.

MONSIEUR:—Occupé exclusivement des affaires particulières de l'Empereur, et retenu constamment aux Tuileries auprès de la personne de sa Majesté, j'ai le regret de ne pouvoir vous assigner un rendezvous selons vos desirs.

Veuillez, je vous prie, me faire connaitre par ecrit, l'objet d'ont vous desirez m'entretenir.

Recevez, Monsieur, l'assurance de ma consideration distinguée.

Le Secretaire de l'Empereur, Chef du Cabinet.

M. R. A. PARRISH,   MOCQUARD.
Grand Hotel du Louvre.

Translation.

PALACE OF THE TUILERIES, 10 Feb., 1857.

Cabinet of the Emperor.

SIR:—Engrossed exclusively with the private affairs of the

Emperor, and detained at the Tuileries constantly at the side of His Majesty, I regret my inability to assign you an interview as you have desired. Have the goodness, I pray you, to apprise me in writing of your object in wishing to see me.

Receive, Sir, the assurance of my distinguished consideration.

The Secretary of the Emperor, Chief of the Cabinet.
MOCQUARD.
Mr. R. A. PARRISH, Grand Hotel du Louvre.

The spirit of evasion which pervades this letter will be more intelligible in the sequel, where it is found that a son of Mr. Mocquard had been heavily bribed by Mirés (together with the Empress, &c., &c,) to defeat the Claimant's appeals to the Emperor.

Stanislaus Hernisz, a German Jew, met the Claimant in the streets of Paris early in May, 1854, accosted him by name, and inquired if it were not he who had submitted to the French Government a Proposition relating to Africa?

The Claimant never having been introduced to him replied, "That is a subject, Sir, into which I must be excused from entering. I wish you a good morning.'

A few weeks later the Claimant received the following

*Letter from Dr. Stanislaus Hernisz, then an Attache of the United States Legation.**

PARIS, 5 June, 1854.
Rue de Ponthieu, Rond Point, No. 10.

DEAR SIR:—I am desirous to see you. I have just come into possession of information of the highest importance to you.

Your recent communication to Mons. T. Ducos, Minister of the Marine, concerning the exploration of the Gold Regions of Senegambia is now under consideration. The opinion which will be formed in relation to it, and the action of the Government will in a great measure depend upon *proper management*.

If you will come to communicate with me in a *frank and liberal* spirit I shall be ready to coöperate with you, and I believe we may have it in our power to bring about a favorable result.

---
* Mr. Jules Levita, another Jew, (and another friend of his Excellency, Mr. Fould,) was at this time Solicitor for the U. S. Legation !!

I shall be at home this evening after 8 o'clock, and shall be glad to see you.
I am truly yours,
STANISLAUS HERNISZ, M. D.
Mr. Parrish, des Etats Unis,
6 Ron Point, Paris.

Astonished at this officiousness the Claimant, being anxious to ascertain the source and nature of the information alleged by Dr. Hernisz, left a card at his address, requesting that he should call on the Claimant at the hour indicated.

The results are substantially set forth in the following

Affidavit of Col. George Mackay.

George Mackay being duly sworn according to law deposes and says:

That he was in Paris, France, during the years 1853 and 1854, and there became acquainted with Mr. Robert A. Parrish, Jr., of Philadelphia, U. S., who had a claim upon the Emperor of France for fifteen millions of francs, the result, as he alleged, of the personal promise of the Emperor to him, at an Extraordinary Audience appointed for the purpose, given as a consideration for making known to the Emperor the existence of Auriferous Territories in Africa, since conquered and annexed to France. This deponent had conversations respecting Mr. Parrish's claim at that time, with the U. S. Ambassador, Mr. Mason, Nicolas Mocquard, (cousin and friend of the private Secretary of the Emperor,) and with the Minister of the Marine, Mr. Ducos, none of whom doubted the integrity of the claim as alleged by Mr. Parrish, or that the Emperor had received him in Extraordinary Audience, and promised him the amount in question. At one time Nicolas Mocquard expected to take an interest in the claim, but was deterred by subsequent circumstances. Dr. Stanislaus Hernisz, a Polish or German Jew, was Attaché or Interpreter of the U. S. Legation in the year 1854, and wrote letters to Mr. Parrish soliciting an interview with him upon the subject of said claim, which letters were shown to this deponent, who was invited by the Claimant to be present at said interview some time in June of said year. Said Hernisz said he had seen the last letter of said Claimant to Mr. Ducos, Minister of the French Marine, that it had created a sensation, and together with the other papers relating to the claim were then in charge of Mr. Fould, Minister of the Imperial Household, that they were endorsed "Proposition de M. Parrish et son Associé;" that a final report would soon be made upon the subject, and that if the Claimant would make it to the interest of said Hernisz to do so, he would take the Claimant to the Bureau of Mr. Fould, exhibit the papers, introduce him to the clerk, and if the Claimant would there communicate any further valuable information, useful to the French in their operations in Africa, said Hernisz would have the report upon said claim moulded into a more favorable shape than it would otherwise assume. All these proposals were promptly declined by said Claimant, who denied that he had an Associé. Dr. Hernisz then spoke of the Emperor in very derogatory terms, and demanded of the Claimant if such were not also his opinions, which the Claimant denied, and replied that he thought it inconceivable that the Emperor could violate his Parole. This deponent introduced the Claimant to the said Chevalier Nicolas Mocquard, who handed the Claimant a letter in French, addressed to the Emperor, for his signature, which the Claimant replaced by one in English which the said Mocquard forwarded to the Emperor. This deponent further heard the said Mocquard detail to the Claimant the time and circumstances attending its delivery to the Emperor, the warm discussion in the Ministry which it occasioned, and saw also the Emperor's reply through the Grand Chamberlain, the Duke of Bassano. The said Mocquard was about to take an interest in said claim had he not been deterred, and from his opportunity of obtaining perfect knowledge as to its value and integrity would not have done so unless convinced that said claim was well founded. In the month of July of said year the said Claimant returned to the United States, having been obliged to borrow of this deponent money to pay his traveling expenses, owing, as he alleged, to the stoppage of his remittances through the intervention of the French Government. Said money was afterwards repaid, and this deponent has no interest in the said claim. Before leaving France said Claimant declared his purpose of procuring, if possible, the aid of the Russian Flag to beat France by arms out of the Kong Mountains of Africa, if said claim was not paid.

From the geological and general attainments of the Claimant he is well qualified for the discussion of subjects such as are embodied in his said Proposition to France.

GEORGE MACKAY.

Sworn and subscribed before me, this 17th day of April, 1867.
THEODORE RITTER.
Notary Public of N. Y. City.

Affidavit of D. Piatt, U. S. Secretary of Legation.

Donn Piatt, being duly sworn according to law, deposes and says, that he was Secretary of the Legation of the United States at Paris, from January, A. D. 1852, until ———, A. D. 185-. Whilst there he became acquainted with Mr. Robert A.

Parrish, Junior, of Philadelphia, who preferred a claim upon the Emperor and Government of France for fifteen millions of francs, originating in some proposition submitted by him to the Emperor, respecting the conquest of Auriferous regions in Africa. Mr. John Y. Mason, the Ambassador of the United States, was acquainted with the fact of Mr. Parrish having been received in Extraordinary Audience by the Emperor in that connection, and that a correspondence was pending between Mr. Parrish and the Ministry. Mr. Parrish wrote to Mr. Mason upon the subject, exhibited this correspondence and solicited his aid to obtain another audience of the Emperor, which was declined. Mr. Stanislaus Hernisz, a German Jew, was an Attaché and Interpreter of the Legation for some time through 1854.

The above statement, prepared for me by Robert A. Parrish, for my signature, I believe to be true, so far as I can recollect.

DONN PIATT.

Sworn to and subscribed before me, this 25th day of October, A. D. 1865. CLINTON KIRBY, [L. s.]
Notary Public Hamilton County, Ohio.

Affidavit of Charles M. Wilkins, M. D.

Charles M. Wilkins, M. D., of the City and State of New York, being duly affirmed according to law, deposes and says, that during part of the years 1853 and 1854, he was in the City of Paris, France, where he frequently met with Mr. Robert A. Parrish, Junior, of the City of Philadelphia aforesaid, and learned the particulars of his claim upon the Emperor and Government of France for fifteen millions of francs, which, as he alleged, was promised to him by the Emperor at an Extraordinary Audience at the Palace of St. Cloud, in consideration of his demonstration to the Emperor of the existence of Auriferous Regions in Africa, similar to California or Australia. This deponent had several conversations with Mr. John Y. Mason, Ambasador of the United States, upon the subject of said claim, who expressed such an intimate knowledge of the facts, and such a faith in its value as to induce this deponent to offer to purchase an interest in said Claim, which he would have done if his funds had been realized in season, pursuant to an agreement in the premises to that effect. This deponent also had conversations with Donn Piatt, then Secretary of the Legation, in reference to said Claim, who expressed a like opinion with said U. S. Minister respecting it. Mr. Mason, the U. S. Minister, expressly stated that the Emperor of France had received Mr. Parrish in audience and promised the sum as above stated, and also said that the French Government

were seriously prosecuting or carrying out Mr. Parrish's scheme. C. M. WILKINS.
Affirmed and subscribed before me this thirtieth day of September, A. D. 1865. W. W. DOUGHERTY,
Alderman.

1857, January 10th.—The Claimant called on Mr. Mason, made new complaints of the persecutions he underwent, and specified amongst the rest the impertinent intrusion in his affairs of Mr. Hernisz, Attaché of the Legation. Mr. Mason at once embarked in an eloquent eulogy of the virtues, learning and honorable qualities of Mr. Hernisz, said he was poor, and although he may have looked for remuneration to the Claimant as the motive for this impertinence, *he could not positively have looked to the other parties.* Mr. Mason at first utterly denied that he, himself, had ever received any hints or intelligence of the Claimant's affairs from the French Government, but presently forgot these remarks so far as to add that a subordinate of the French Foreign Office had informed him that a Commission had been appointed by the Imperial Government in 1853 or 54, (comprising savants from the Academy of France, at the head of which was a friend ot Mr. Hernisz,) to investigate and report upon the Claimant's Proposition. In fact, the U. S. Embassy, during the whole term of Mr. Mason's service was a virtual Legation from Jerusalem, and represented simply the coming Southern Confederacy and the Jews. When Mr. Piatt resigned the Secretaryship he was succeeded by Messrs. Calhoun and Wise, (both traitors,) and the northern United States were ignored. Hence it was, that when Mr. Buchanan was inaugurated, the Emperor, before the full assembled court, seizing Mr. Mason by *both hands* one day, expressed *the hope* that in the transitions going on at home he would still be allowed *to represent his country!*

On the 26th of Dec., 1856, the civilized world had been horror-stricken by one of the most audacious assassinations on record. Mr. Sibour, Archbishop of Paris, the highest and most powerful ecclesiastic in France, was assassinated in Church in the midst of his functions, by an assassin who had been *nominally* officiating as a Priest in the Imperial Chapel of the Tuileries! The Moniteur, the official journal of France, a few days later, gave the details of the crime, and said that the assassin had lately been in Holland and Belgium, and had also frequented the Bibliotheque Imperiale at Paris. The Claimant had been at all these places *at the same precise time.* He was obliged to retire from the Imperial Library altogether on account of the sinister presence and manner of this fiend. The Claimant was warned against him. The wretched Archbishop was believed to have been the medium of this warning.

Letter of Mr. Parrish to his Father, with enclosures for the U. S. Secretary of State.

PARIS, 13 January, 1857.

DEAR FATHER:—My previous letters have given you reiterated hints of intrigues, (instigated by high official influence, and of a more or less ominous import,) which have latterly enveloped me in incessant anxieties. The details have been withheld; but as it is now proper that you should be more minutely advised, and inasmuch as a statement of one instance will suffice to illustrate them all, I will proceed to give the facts of a single case.

Madame Baudoux Cottaint—the landlady at my late residence, No. 256 Rue St. Honoré—hearing me speak of taking lessons in French, begged leave to present *a widow* of her acquaintance, a most deserving lady, who possessed peculiar qualifications. Accordingly Madame Dumont née Ortrie, was introduced: lately from Tours, and visiting Paris ostensibly to secure a place in an Orphans' Asylum (lately instituted by Her Majesty) for two *orphans*, maintained and educated by her, Madame Dumont, for years, under peculiar hardships. Madame Dumont was about thirty-five years of age, pretty, of good address, but with a bad moral expression of countenance. I declined making any engagement with her. Other persons subsequently sent to me by appointment were dismissed by my landlady, before reaching my door, under the allegation that I was "out," or had already made an engagement. The application of Madame D. continued to be pressed, notwithstanding my plainly pronounced objections. In a week or so, she came and domiciled herself in the room adjoining my apartments, and thenceforth (with the undisguised connivance of Madame Cottaint) thrust herself continually upon my notice. When returning home, late at night, my key (instead of being in her own hands, as previously,) was entrusted by Madame Cottaint to Madame Dumont, who, unsolicited, and indeed in spite of my remonstrances, would persistently enter my rooms at midnight *to light my candles!* Against these proceedings, I repeatedly protested, plainly perceiving that they enveloped an intrigue. It was utterly in vain. My manner, however, was always strictly polite, never over-stepping the bounds of the most fastidious decorum.

One day I had a conversation in my own rooms with my tailor—the doors being shut—respecting a thick overcoat to wear to Sweden, whither I meditated making a hurried journey. A day or two afterwards a stranger was shown into my apartments by Madame Cottaint, with a coat heavily lined with fur, alleging that it was new, not suited to the gentleman for whom it was made, and that being rejected, he would sell it to me very low. I observed marks of *use* upon it, and declined it, although he protested it was new. A day or two later I learned that Madame Dumont, the pretended widow, had a husband, a jealous, violent and vulgar brute; that she was living apart from him, and that the pretended *new fur coat* belonged to him! Moreover, the *orphans* were his children!! Should I unguardedly have bought the coat, he would probably have assailed me in a murderous manner, in some public place, and whilst charging me with abducting his wife and family, point in justification of his violence to his very coat upon my back.

Immediately upon the discovery of Madame Dumont's true character and objects, I left in the middle of my term, obtaining (by stratagem) from my landlady a letter, admitting that the entrusting my key to strangers, and intercepting my visitors, had been on my part a subject of complaint.

Now the foregoing (omitting innumerable details) is a faint picture of one, out of a number, of the most ingenious and diabolical intrigues that were ever attempted. They were, moreover, upheld and instigated by high official influence; inasmuch as the Minister of War visited Madame Dumont; the Bishop of Palmier gave her a strong and eloquent recommendation; and she was in correspondence with the Chief of Police of the City of Paris, as I accidentally saw, by an official letter written to her from his Bureau.

When amidst scenes like these, my trunks and letter books (both secured by Brahmah locks,) are opened and examined, not once but often, I think it full time to give way to a sentiment of anxiety. That these intrigues are the common and practiced expedients of this government, and that they are meant to humiliate, injure and destroy me, I do not for one instant doubt. And when in superaddition to all this, I remember that Doctor Hernisz, Attaché to the U. S. Legation at Paris in 1854, was actually employed by Mr. Fould, the Minister of State, to approach me as a spy with infamous propositions, and actually wrote me a letter (which I still hold) in the same strain, I cannot and do not question that my reputation and my interests are alike exposed to many and formidable perils; the more, that there is not a spot upon the globe whose atmosphere is so absolutely putrid with perjury as that of Paris. For these reasons I earnestly entreat you, if possible, to procure me an appointment as Attaché to this Legation, and whilst my general character, attainments and habits would amply warrant the appointment, (as papers in the Department of State at Washington, accompanying my application for a Secretaryship of Legation, will testify,) I think I may confidently look for it on the broad grounds of justice and humanity.

Pray hurry to Washington, taking copies of my correspondence with the French Government and Mr. Mason, and address yourself *solely to Mr. Marcy*, whose courage and integrity I know. If it can be done consistently, he will do it, I am sure.

With much and painful solicitude
I remain affectionately yours,
ROBERT.

R. A. PARRISH, Esq , Philadelphia, Pa.

Letter to Mr. Marcy, Intercepted and Cut Off by Gen. J. A. Thomas, Assistant Secretary of State, enclosing Correspondence with the French Government. Sent with the foregoing.

PARIS, 13 January, 1857, }
Grand Hotel du Louvre. }

SIR :—The accompanying correspondence will put your Excellency in possession of the more material facts touching a negotiation, curious in its character, and of rather unusual magnitude, remaining still incomplete, between His Majesty, the Emperor of France, and myself. Of late, through a tissue of crafty artifices, inseparable, perhaps, from such a case, it has involved me in complications which menace, as I seriously believe, not my liberty or my life alone, but even my reputation. I deem it, therefore, full time to make your Excellency privy to the truth, and at once to invoke your official intervention. In so doing, I look for nothing further than is implied in the respectful expression of a request that his Excellency, Mr. Mason, should be empowered to give me an appointment as Attaché to the Legation of the United States here. The whole object of this request is my personal security; my more urgent reasons respecting which will be detailed by the bearer of this letter.

It is proper to remark, however, that an application to the same effect, made by me to his Excellency, in the year 1853, was first conditionally promised to be granted, (to wit: upon the condition that the French Ministry should admit by correspondence the existence of my negotiation,) but afterwards, upon the fulfillment of that condition, was demurred to. From natural sentiments of delicacy the application was immediately abandoned, nor has it ever been renewed. A few days ago, however, in a conversation with him on other matters, relating to my negotiation, he gave expression to his belief that the late "Diplomatic and Consular Bill" restrained his interference in my affairs in any way!*

Inasmuch as a rude hand laid by a foreign power upon an American ship, or upon the most insignificant individual or article which it might contain, (and whether thus imposed either by intrigue or by violence,) would call forth the whole defensive authority of the Legation, I am at a loss to understand why through diplomatic niceties my life or fortunes should be flung a prey to the diabolical intrigues of this court, noted throughout the world (up to the present regime) for its despotic habits and thinly disguised rapacity. What, moreover, constitutes the peculiar gravamen of my position, is the fact that certain official persons, from motives only too apparent, throwing themselves as a rampart before the throne, blockade all access by letter or otherwise.

Were it not that my well-founded anxiety for the future is great, I would be far from pressing my request, as above stated, against the rather strongly pronounced hesitation of an Ambassador; but as I well know that his Excellency advances no personal reasons for objecting, and only awaits the legitimate faculty of complying, I respectfully entreat (if it be in your power to bestow it) that such a faculty may be accorded to him. I feel the more strongly warranted in submitting this request from the fact that I conceive myself to personate an important question of right and justice, to which your Excellency cannot be insensible, and which I take to be preëminently a topic of interest to the American people. In addressing myself to your Excellency, I am addressing them.

I have the honor to remain, with unfeigned consideration and respect,
Your obedient servant,
R. A. PARRISH, JR.,
of Philadelphia.

To His Excellency, W. L. MARCY,
U. S. Sec'y of State, Washington, D. C.

Mad. Cottaint to Mr. Parrish. [*Translation.*] *Enclosed.*

PARIS, 19 Dec., 1856.

MR. PARRISH:—I reiterate here the assurance I have already given you verbally, that you have accused me of no other wrongs than the interception of an umbrella, and that I committed your key to the custody of strangers.

Receive, Sir, my earnest salutations,
VVE BAUDOUX COTTAINT.

* This Bill was corruptly passed through Congress.

These letters (as detailed by affidavits on file at Washington) never reached Mr. Marcy. They were intercepted in the ante-room of the Department of State, by Gen. J. A. Thomas, then Assistant Secretary, who, by various pretences, adroitly cut off the approaches of the Claimant's representative. The insidious villainy of Gen. Thomas was but poorly requited. He went soon afterwards to Paris, where *he happened to eat something which disagreed with him, and died.*

On the 15th of Jan'y, 1857, the Claimant was invited to dinner by Mr. Brewster, (formerly Dentist to Louis Philippe,) who had promised to forward a message to the Emperor. The dinner proved a mere ambuscade. The confidence of the Claimant, in connection with this subject, was openly violated in presence of the company, and intrigues set on foot at the time to his very serious detriment. He was also charged before the company with having made statements which he had not made, and was pestered to authorize a simpleton who was present to settle the Claim for the half of what he might get;—a proposition which was rejected.

1857, Jan. and Feb.—The Claimant's name was registered in the Audience Book, during these two months in vain.

1857, Feb. 12.—The persecutions to which the Claimant was exposed during the whole time of his residence in Paris at length reached such a point as to indicate that his life was in continual peril; whereupon, as the Emperor could not be approached for protection, either by letter or otherwise, and being further warned that if he remained in Paris he would be implicated in the coming Orsini Opera House Conspiracy, (which was a mere trick of the French police,) the Claimant on advice of friends, was again constrained to withdraw from France.

On his return to the United States he was also beset with numerous intrigues, chiefly through the instrumentality of lewd women, paid for the purpose, as had been the case in Paris. Unfounded slanders (an engine of great power in France) were also actively employed against him. Mr. Buchanan (then President of the United States,) entertained an emissary of Mr. Fould at the White House, established an *en-*

tente cordiale with the French Government,* publicly asserted that the Claimant had misconducted himself grossly in Paris, and exerted the whole weight and influence of his great office to defeat this Claim. Under his authority the forgery of the Claimant's papers in the United States Department of State took place, preliminary to the printing by the United States Senate of the "List of Claims on Foreign Governments," which was gotten up for the express purpose of creating a forged record, thereby to discharge the honor of the French Emperor from that infamy which a true record would have disclosed. Perhaps the strongest convictions of the integrity and justice of this Claim have been engendered, however, by these very corrupt practices, which virtually confess that there is no resource of sophistry and no principle of justice which can be marshaled to crush or gainsay it. The fact, moreover, that Mr. Buchanan knew from the beginning the history of the subject, having perused and approved the Memorial of the Claimant at Wheatland, in 1853, and followed it up with a sordid avidity all the while he was in office, attaches a peculiar turpitude to his unprincipled proceedings.

Amongst other outrages of which the Claimant was the object, was one which is hinted at in the following letters:

Letter to the Ex-Mayor of Philadelphia.

PHILADELPHIA, 2 October, 1860.

SIR:—Whilst you were Mayor of Philadelphia I had occasion to call your attention to a plot which, as I believe, was on foot for my ruin, implicating amongst other persons Mrs. ——, (the paramour of the notorious Col. Cross,) and then residing at No. —— Chestnut Street.† There were at the time three Frenchmen lodging with her, one of whom was a Mr. Worthabet, a soi-disant son of a Protestant Bishop of Syria.

You instituted an official inquiry into the matter, and whilst you saw enough to satisfy yourself that I was right in my interpretation of it, you thought the evidence within your reach would scarcely suffice to warrant a prosecution.

As I am again assailed by some of these parties, will you have the great kindness now to verify in writing this, my statement of the facts? For my present as well as future

---

*See New York Herald, July 5th and 9th, 1858.
†The celebrated perjurer, Conover, was also an habitué of these premises.

protection, I desire to retain some evidence of occurrences so extraordinary.

I have the honor to be yours very truly,
R. A. PARRISH, Jr.

RICHARD VAUX, Esq., Philada.

Reply of the Hon. Richard Vaux, Ex-Mayor.

PHILADELPHIA, Oct. 2, 1860.

DEAR SIR:—Your note of this morning is respectfully acknowledged.

Whilst I was Mayor of Philadelphia you laid before me a complaint, which you had against certain parties whom you regarded as conspiring to give you annoyance, and from whom you entertained fear of serious injury. The proof, or at least a large part of it, I then examined, but gave it as my opinion that it did not amount to sufficient evidence on which to found legal proceedings. I cannot now recall the date. You may be able to supply that from your own papers.

Very respectfully,
RICHARD VAUX.

R. A. PARRISH, Jr., Esq.

His Honor's investigations resulted in a stampede of these parties.

The thrice-hellish wickedness of the French Government is scarcely capable of belief. A favorite "fetch" is to quarantine its victim from the society of women for a length of time, (which, with their vast power, is not difficult,) then to propagate rumors that his passions are unnatural, intemperate and utterly ungovernable, so that "public opinion" will ultimately justify results. He is then impudently and ingeniously besieged without cessation by lewd women, leprous with the most fearful forms of infection, and if they can succeed in infecting him he is arrested on any pretended charge, and kept incarcerated without medical aid until he is virtually eaten up with disease. As soon as he is beyond the reach of earthly hope or remedy, he is enlarged with hypocritical manifestations of tenderness and humanity. The credulous multitude accept his fate as the legitimate consequence of his "ungovernable passions," little imagining that crime is the practiced instrument of their Government for the achievement of any of its ends. If the veil which screens it were to fall—the horror inspiring visage of Medusa would be revealed.

Americans are less capable of comprehending the moral structure of the French Government than almost any other people. As their own Government embodies the most exalted principles of liberty and justice, they incline intuitively to accredit similar principles to France. The radical moral antagonism of the two systems is not perceived. Ours is a system of pure justice. Theirs of pure selfishness and iron-clad violence. The inauguration of justice would dissipate the French Empire in a day—the inauguration of liberty, in an instant. It is not generally known that two hundred thousand men vanished from society by the Coup d'Etat; and that the very champions of republicanism, whose franchises had elevated the present Emperor to the Presidency, forthwith suffered a political, if not a physical assassination. Many were shipped to Cayenne and other penal colonies, where they expired miserably. Multitudes perished in prison from unexplained causes, of which, infection and the knife were the most convenient, usual, and probable. The greater part were crowded as conscripts into the army, and sent on foreign duty to Africa, Mexico, Cochin-China, &c., &c. Assassination, however, carried to the precision and perfection of a science, is an *organic function of the Imperial Government*. It could not have survived without it. Just before the Coup d'Etat a refractory General, whose fidelity was feared, was stabbed in the Emperor's presence at the Tuileries, and the infamy hushed up as an angry quarrel *between officers*. This the Emperor, of course, most graciously condoned. The assassination of Sibour, the Archbishop of Paris, was clearly a political act. There was no other way to get rid of him. Whilst he lived, the Empire drew a bated breath. Appointed during the Republic, and known to possess an unaffected sympathy toward it, he never could acquire the confidence of its immolators. It was indispensable, moreover, to the efficiency and repose of the new regime that this office—the most influential in the Empire—should be filled by an incumbent of unequivocal fidelity. The precious villain who succeeded him was of that exact stamp. No more supple and inhuman Jesuit ever lived. Since then the Empire has slept in peace. The blow which struck Sibour was not, as pretended, that of a fanatic and a madman. On the contrary, the whole method of the blow was evidently that of a practiced assassin of the first class, and of the very highest range of experience; of just such an assassin—in other words—as should preside at the Imperial Chapel of the Tuileries, which had long been his post! His office is, in fact, an important adjunct of the Empire.

The Emperor says:—L'Empire c'est la Paix. Punch punningly says: L'Empire c'est l'Epée, meaning more properly le Couteau, which is a much truer word than is often used in jest.

Letter of Mr. Parrish to Mr. Buchanan, President of the United States, (from the Philadelphia Evening Bulletin, Aug. 24, 1860.)

PHILADELPHIA, August 15, 1860.

SIR:—It is my desire to visit and remain some time in France, to consummate a negotiation with the Emperor, which has been pending between us for the past seven years. I invite your Excellency's attention again to this unusual subject, from the demonstrated impossibility of accomplishing my purpose without the coöperation of my own Government; the all sufficient evidence of which fact will be made apparent in the course of this letter.

The following letter, written over a year ago, to the Secretary of State, sets forth many of the pertinent grounds upon which this present application is preferred, with the truth of all which your Excellency is already thoroughly acquainted.

Letter to General Cass.

PHILADELPHIA, December 2, 1858.

SIR:—I am a native citizen of the United States, and have a claim upon the Government of France for fifteen millions of francs, long since due and payable, and for the payment of which, as I am led to understand, a special appropriation was made, by an Imperial Decree, dated July 16, 1854. This appropriation has never reached me, and my intercourse with the Emperor, either personally or by letter, has been totally cut off. My sojourn in Paris, moreover, with a view to the prosecution of this claim, has been rendered impossible. My letters and funds in the French Post-office have been habitually arrested and delayed; my residence, my trunks, my books and papers, have been subjected to incessant invasions, and a multiplication of intrigues have been employed to compromise my repose and render a stay there fatal to my comfort, if not indeed to my liberty or my life. The Ambassador of the United States, with a knowledge of these facts, has refused to extend to me the shelter of the legation, and constrained me to make a formal appeal for protection to the Executive at Washington.

The claim is based upon the Emperor's parole, which was pledged to me, in consideration of certain evidence demonstrating the existence of a gold field, similar to that of California, and in a region accessible to the arms of France, which I had the distinguished honor of bringing to his notice. It was to become payable as soon as the authority of France was established in any part of the territory indicated. This condition has been long since fulfilled, and the French Government is actually employed in working the gold mines.

A history of the claim (commencing with a proposition from me to the Government of the United States) is detailed in the accompanying correspondence, which I respectfully request may be filed with the other papers already left by me in the hands of the President.

I have the honor to remain, with distinguished consideration, your obedient servant,

R. A. PARRISH, JR.

To His Excellency, Hon. LEWIS CASS,
Secretary of State, Washington, D. C.

A proposition to acquire and annex this same gold field was submitted by me to my own government in the year 1853, and, as your Excellency is also well aware, was not carried out, mainly through the inability of the Administration to execute the scheme with adequate secrecy. The "Memorial" then laid before the President (which I had also the honor to exhibit to your Excellency at Wheatland, prior to our voyages to Europe in 1853, and which is now in the possession of the French Government,) was the chief basis upon which that proposition rested. Upon its submission to the Minister of the French Marine, pursuant to my extraordinary audience with His Majesty, its theories were adopted as axiomatically true, and an expeditionary force of over thirteen vessels and twenty-five hundred men, dispatched for the conquest of the territory. Following the foreshadowings of my Memorial, the French power has been extended from Senegal (then a petty village, peopled chiefly with barbarians, and with but a nominal commerce,) across the Kong Mountains to Timbuctoo, and is ineradicably planted in all the upper valley of the Niger. In fact, save Liberia, Morocco, Tunis, Tripoli, Egypt, and the petty European posts on the west coast—few of which will probably long survive—the whole continent of Africa, north of the line, has become an integral part of the French Empire. The portion of it which is traversed by the Kong Mountains "contains the richest gold deposits in the world."

The passage of some two hundred Imperial Decrees (an index to which accompanies my correspondence), French Treaties with many European Powers, and a vast Colonial Administration in Senegal, still engaged in the prosecution of my scheme, testify, in some slight degree, to its national value and intrinsic magnificence! Indeed, so just were my reasonings, and so felicitous their application by His Majesty, that, since the working of the mines (which are a government monopoly), the Emperor has been coining annually, *in gold only*, over five hundred millions of francs!—a sum greater than the aggregate gold coinage of the United States, Great Britain and Russia (all of which have affluent gold fields), and not only greater than that of Spain when carried by Columbus to the culmination of her power, but even greater than the antecedent coinage of any nation upon the globe! For this unparalleled opulence, the Emperor is indebted exclusively to my demonstrations. The foregoing statistics are derived from the Report of His Excellency, Mr. Magne, French Minister of Finance, who further states, that for the first nine months only, of 1858, the French imports of gold *exceeded the exports* by three hundred and seventy-six millions (376,000,000) of francs!—facts which abundantly manifest the justice of compensating me, even if I claimed the full measure of the Emperor's promised munificence. But this, however, I do not desire. His Majesty's confidence, as well as my own, has been greatly abused in the premises, or this claim (however small relatively) would never have attained its present magnitude. The Emperor even promised that I should receive for a term of years (discharged of the costs of the enterprise) one-half the product of the mines, now and for some years back, as I have already stated, exceeding one hundred millions of dollars per annum; a flood of munificence which I declined, from its very magnitude alone. My fixed purpose from the beginning was to limit the compensation within practical bounds, that I might evade some of that official cupidity which I knew would otherwise surround, embarrass, and assail me.

This apprehension was but too prophetically true. No sooner did his Excellency, Mr. Fould, Minister of the Imperial Household, learn the nature of my errand—that I would treat with the Emperor only, and even with him only on his promise of some sufficient requital—than his Excellency insisted that I should receive from the Emperor a sum three times greater than I desired, and that one-third thereof should be appropriated to himself. To giving him one-third I entertained no possible objection, and cheerfully acceded—although my maximum was five millions of francs. My objection to more colossal sums was strong and earnest, and I withstood his tyrannical exactions until it became manifest that acquiescence was indispensable to success. Immediately after my unwilling consent, an audience with the Emperor was appointed, whereupon His Majesty (unconscious of the sordid purposes of his Minister) promised me the sum which that officer had prompted. He also promised me a written Traité, to be drawn up by the Minister of the Marine, as an unsolicited guarantee of his august parole.

A few weeks later, when the expedition had sailed, and this Traité was on the brink of consummation, his Excellency, Mr. Fould, astounded me by proposing one of his creatures as my Associate in that instrument! Stupified at this new usurpation, I hesitated to comply, for compliance was ruin. Upon this, his Excellency abruptly broke with me, and has pursued me with implacable hostility ever since. He was even so unscrupulous as shortly afterwards to write me an *official letter*, in which he mentions my CO-PARTNER, as if a person actually avowed and recognized by me; well knowing at that time, and at all times, that I stood entirely alone, both as the author and negotiator of the scheme An invitation to breakfast with His Majesty was intercepted or defeated; rumors that I was insane, and slanders the most injurious were immediately propagated to my prejudice, and wherever his Excellency's power could reach, I became a caitiff! All this, however, is but a confession of my rights. I had traveled in Europe before the date of this negotiation, at which time I had no claim to three millions of dollars, and accordingly heard no rumors of my insanity, nor did I detect high official personages, on either side of the Atlantic, industriously employed in defrauding and denouncing me. *It was then unprofitable.*

During my last three visits to Paris I was placed under the strictest surveillance; my efforts to see the Emperor, or even to communicate with him by letter, were altogether baffled. One letter only *seems* to have reached him, and brought a reply. When in December, 1856, I was presented at Court, His Majesty entered into conversation with me, and willingly promised me a private audience, with a view to some final arrangement, but before this could be brought about I was again expelled from France by the strategy of Mr. Fould. To such a length indeed was his Excellency's enterprise extended, that even in America I have felt its effects. Amongst other things, the synopsis of my claim, furnished by me in writing to the Department of State, was afterwards corrupted by his emissaries, and went into print [in Senate Ex. Doc., No. 18, 35th Congress, 2d Session, p. 16,] as a claim "resting on a *verbal agreement with himself*, as Minister of Finance," whereas I had written "that the claim was based upon the Emperor's parole." This most unprincipled metamorphosis of a Government record, and so flatly at variance with the truth, is thus made to wear my apparent sanction! But I here denounce it to your Excellency, as not the greatest of those frauds and outrages which I have been compelled to suffer in this connection for the past seven years

When your Excellency reverts to the barefaced efforts of Mr. Talleyrand (Minister of Foreign Affairs of the French Government, in 1793,) to extort fifty thousand pounds sterling from the Ambassadors of the United States, "for the pockets of the Ministry," [as appears in the American State Papers, published by order of Congress, Washington, folio, 1832, pp. 158 to 168, and 229 to 238, Vol. II, Foreign Relations.] it will cease to be incredible, perhaps, that when three millions of dollars are in question, his Excellency, Mr. Fould, should follow to-day that distinguishing example! So glaring, indeed, were these facts, as to have challenged from the American Secretary of State the remark—[ibid. p. 230]—"that the sensation which these details irresistibly excite, is that of astonishment at the unparalleled effrontery of Mr. Talleyrand."

Being at once the wealthiest and most powerful officer of the Imperial Government, no one with greater hope of impunity than Mr. Fould could venture to abuse the Imperial confidence, or sell the Imperial honor for a price. But Napoleon III. is as little likely as Napoleon I. to tolerate such practices; and as Talleyrand was constrained to deny and retract his offence, so will his Excellency, Mr. Fould, in my case, if the evidence in my possession shall ever be investigated. Indeed, it was but recently that the noble pride and honorable sensibility of His Majesty were conspicuously manifested on a kindred subject. In his letter to Mr. Persigny [of St. Cloud, 25th July, 1860,] he says: "Let us understand one another in good faith, like honest men, as we are, and not like thieves, who desire to cheat each other." I take pleasure in believing that these are his genuine sentiments, and that, whilst enjoying the unbounded opulence which I have flung into his hands (which alone was wanting to consolidate his dynasty and render him the most potent of Monarchs), he could not falter in the least of those pledges, by which such stupendous benefits were obtained. He has been deceived—as I have been—by the Minister of his Household and my alleged Associate.

In view then of the foregoing, I respectfully solicit an appointment as Attaché to the Legation of the United States at Paris, in order that I may reside there unmolested, until I can see His Majesty and bring this negotiation to an end; also, that instructions be given to his Excellency, Mr. Faulkner, to give me all necessary protection, and to procure me an early audience of the Emperor. I owe no debts in France, and have no other affairs there than this.

These requests, be it clearly understood, do not embody a desire that the Government of the United States *should assume the prosecution of this Claim,* nor supplant me in any part of the negotiation. It is certain that no one could conduct it so advantageously as myself, and that a brief interview with His Majesty would enable us to arrive at a satisfactory conclusion: the more, that I still have intelligence (which I am ready to surrender to him) that will give a value to his new colony fifty-fold greater than all the fund in question between us.

This appointment is respectfully asked upon a two-fold ground; first, as my undoubted right, and second, as an act of grace and duty, which it would be inequitable to refuse, and which I am sure your Excellency would be gratified to perform.

The several Legations of the United States are expressly created to protect the lives, liberties and interests of American citizens in foreign lands—more especially in lands like France, where writs of habeas corpus are unknown, and Liberty has no existence. Whether the person (as in the case of Martin Koszta), or his estate (as in the case of the French Spoliation Claims above alluded to), is the subject of invasion, it has been the long established usage of the Government to intervene in their defence. And not only does my case combine the equity of both these instances—but, in view of the groundless arrest and homicide of Mr. Morley (an American, who had a contract with the French Government), during my late residence in Paris; of the impossibility also of my own unmolested residence there, without the aid I seek; and still more, from the fact, that all the citizens of the United States combined have not so large a claim upon that government, and so urgent a necessity for protection as myself, your Excellency could scarcely hesitate to grant my request.

The Diplomatic and Consular Bill of 1855, which (without the allegation of a reason) abolished the office of Attaché, was one of those cases of improvident legislation which, in the nature of things, occasionally transpire, but which, in the opinion of the Attorney General of the United States, was—in so far as respects its creation or amotion of diplomatic offices—*absolutely null and void.* His judgment, to this effect, reiterated in various shapes, upon pages 9, 10, 13, 17, 21, 28, 30, 33 and 37, of his printed opinion (which is adopted by the Department of State as its rule of interpretation) is clear and positive; thus leaving your Excellency just as free to make such an appointment as before the date of this nugatory enactment—a freedom which (in consimili casu) has been exerted in various other appointments under that Act of much greater importance.

Moreover, in your Excellency's speech, from the steps of the White House, delivered on the 9th ultimo, I notice the following unanswerable argument in my favor: "Well, now, *any set of principles which will deprive you of your property* is against the very essence of republican government, and to that extent makes you a slave." In this language I perceive a virtual admission that your Excellency's *power*, and your Excellency's *right*, to give me the aid I seek, will be exercised in my favor, particularly as any hesitation to do so would be to deprive me of my property, and (however unintentionally) would be actively to promote the hostile and fraudulent policy of Mr. Fould.

Our present Ambassador, Mr. Faulkner, well knowing the fact of my frequent journeys to, and long residence in Europe, and my colloquial acquaintance with several of its languages, especially with the Spanish and the French, has already expressed his cheerful acquiescence in my wishes, as here set forth, and I am certain would do anything for the interests of his countrymen, which was warranted by considerations of duty and of honor. And, in conclusion, I cannot believe that your Excellency could think it becoming the dignity and justice, either of my own or of the Imperial Government, that, after the great expense and inconvenience which I have already undergone in this remarkable affair, I should be put to any further procrastination which you could so readily prevent.

I have the honor to be your Excellency's obedient servant,
ROBERT A. PARRISH, Jr.
To His Excellency JAMES BUCHANAN,
President of the U. S., Washington, D. C.

[This Letter elicited no other notice than a storm of angry falsehoods, not loud, but deep.]

One of the most beautiful women in America, who had been fluttering around the U. S. Legation at London, during Mr. Buchanan's incumbency (a virtual attaché), and who, as *she* said, had traveled from Memphis to New York at the expense of Baron Rothschild, was staying alone, in 1861, at a hotel on Broadway. She frequently invited the Claimant to drive out with her in a sumptuous carriage, placed by the Baron at her disposition. Her invitations were uniformly declined. Once only he was prevailed on to call on her, which, as he had unsettled business with her husband, was in a measure necessary. Although he had sent up his card, he was unexpectedly ushered by the servant into her bedroom! She was in decided dishabille! Although his visit was purposely brief, it was interrupted under circumstances to inspire the fixed belief, not only that some fatal mischief was then intended for him, but that Mr. Buchanan himself was not entirely unaware of it. The plot failed. The lady is since divorced, and lives in Europe. Mr. Buchanan also stood in the shadow of a second and very similar scheme.

Mr. Buchanan (whatever opinions to the contrary may have once prevailed) was capable of the very lowest order of villainy. It was he, who, by a perjured violation of his oath of office, during his last term in the U. S. Senate, betrayed their discussions in Executive Sessions to the New York Herald, which led to the arrest and imprisonment of Mr. Nugent. As soon as Mr. Buchanan became President, he appointed Mr. Nugent to a lucrative Indian Agency on the Pacific Slope, and sent him into exile. A noted agent of Louis Napoleon, even at that early day, was mixed up in the affair; but Mr. Buchanan was not then the object of suspicion.

It is also well known in Philadelphia, that on the threshold of the late rebellion, he sought in vain to corrupt a sturdy and distinguished patriot of that city by the offer of "ten thousand dollars and a foreign mission," if he would renounce the cause of the people *and unite in the crime of treason*. Many other attendant circumstances criminate the wretch in assisting his Cabinet to organize the rebellion and to deluge this fair land with blood. That they cordially coöperated with him (except Gen. Cass, then in his dotage,) will further appear, perhaps, from the following letters. The doctrine, which is expressed in the words—falsus in uno, falsus in omnibus, (if ever applicable) indubitably applies to him with great force.

Mr. Parrish to Mr. Cobb, enclosing his Letter to the President.

PHILADELPHIA, August 27, 1860.

SIR:—I beg leave to solicit your Excellency's perusal of the accompanying copy of my late letter to the President, (published in the Bulletin of this city, on Friday last,) and relating to my Claim upon the Emperor of France.

Apart from its importance to myself, the palpable questions of equity presented by it, and the growing historical moment of the subject generally, would seem to challenge for it your grave consideration.

If, moreover, my appeals for justice could (through your

Excellency's aid,) be heard and granted, I can only say that
my acknowledgments would be unceasing.
I have the honor to remain, with great consideration, your
obedient servant.   R. A. PARRISH, Jr.,
 No. 1305 Arch St.
To His Excellency, Hon. HOWELL COBB,
 Secretary of the Treasury, Washington, D. C.

Reply of Mr. Cobb.

TREASURY DEPARTMENT, Aug. 28, 1860.

SIR:—Your letter of the 27th inst. is received. I beg leave to state that the claim against France, stated in your letter to the President, is not within the cognizance or jurisdiction of this Department, and therefore it is not within my lawful power to take any steps in the matter.

Very respectfully, your obedient servant,
 HOWELL COBB,
 Secretary of the Treasury.
ROBERT A. PARRISH, Jr., Esq.,
 No. 1305 Arch Street, Philadelphia, Pa.

Rejoinder of Mr. Parrish.

PHILADELPHIA, Aug. 29, 1860.

SIR:—In response to mine of the 27th inst., (enclosing you my published letter to the President of the 15th,) I am this moment honored by your Excellency's favor of the 28th. It apprises me "that my claim against France, stated in my letter to the President, is not within the cognizance or jurisdiction of your office, and therefore it is not within your lawful power to take any steps in the matter."

For the prompt attention of this reply, I tender my sincere acknowledgments; but with your Excellency's leave, would desire to submit for your further consideration a respectful expression of my true meaning, in then addressing you. It seems to have been misconceived, and was intended, *as this explanation also,* for the whole Cabinet.

Whilst as a lawyer, I am well aware, that neither the Laws nor the Constitution of the United States, invest your Excellency (in your separate capacity of Secretary of the Treasury) with power to take initial steps in the premises, yet we all know, that the unvarying usage of the Government since its foundation, warrants the belief that your Excellency's opinion in this matter will be called for. In other words, I take it for granted, that the President will refer the subject to his Cabinet.

As one of the "Constitutional advisers" of the President, (popularly so-called,) your Excellency, in common with the several Heads of Department, meet that high officer in Cabinet

Councils, as often commonly as twice a week, to confer upon such questions as he may submit. Now, neither the Constitution nor the laws directly authorize these Councils; but from the exalted sanction of Washington's example, followed by that of every one of his successors, they have come to be regarded as essential a part of the working machinery of the government as the meetings of Congress itself. Upon the hypothesis, therefore, that the President would submit the subject of my printed letter to the Cabinet, I addressed myself to your Excellency on the 27th inst., *in your capacity of Cabinet Councillor;* in which capacity you can, and I trust you will, assist me in a most substantial manner. If, with the noble devotion to truth and justice, for which I believe your Excellency to be distinguished, you declare in the Cabinet Councils, THAT NOT TO AID ME, IS TO OPPOSE ME; that not to support me with the whole power of the government, is to justify and advocate the policy of Mr. Fould; and moreover, that every man in the realm of newspapers must sooner or later know of this, I am sure that your Excellency's coöperation will be most potent, particularly where you may with the utmost candor add, that if all my small petition be granted, no possible harm can come to any honest man. For grievances like mine there ought to be a remedy; and it should be supplied with alacrity. If I am in the wrong let me take my fate; but if I am in the right—in the name of common decency—let me not appeal to my own government in vain. My claim, as previously stated, is for 15,000,000 of francs, promised to me by the Emperor himself, upon conditions which are long since fulfilled.

My complaint is, that my rights have been most tyrannically abused, my large property embezzled or confiscated, my liberty and even my life exposed to peril, and my residence in France for the settlement of this claim rendered impracticable, without the sanctity of a diplomatic appointment. In my humble judgment, if a case such as I thus represent does not engage the earnest attention of the Cabinet, and challenge the prompt and willing intervention of the Government, then there is but little use in having a Cabinet, and still less in having Foreign Legations. Nor do I stand by any means alone in this opinion. Our Legations, unless practically useful, will dwindle (as the offices of Attaché themselves) into mere names; if, indeed, they do not invoke the legitimate scoff of the whole country. They don't go abroad in a sycophantic and eleemosynary spirit, to sue for popularity or favors. Accredited by a practical Government, they go to do their duty, which (in the interest of the national honor) it is to be hoped, is simply to ask for what is right; and with a manly courage and honorable independence befitting the noblest Republic on the globe to countenance no replies that are incompatible with justice. Upon any other theory of their existence, the American people would sweep them all away. When a petty schooner is "searched" (without loss or harm), or when a drunken sailor is arrested in a foreign port, the Legations of the United States, acting in the sacred name of liberty, do not deem it beneath their dignity to exert their whole protective power for the security of the parties. If then, where 15,000,000 of francs are at issue, and the intrigues which are inevitable in such cases are aiming at the life and liberty of an American citizen, his government decline to intervene, such refusal would be tantamount to a public proclamation that Americans thenceforth may be pillaged with impunity.

The intervention which I solicit, is an appointment to the office of Attaché to our Embassy in Paris; an office which, under our practice, *has neither salary nor duties*, and is of no value, except for the immediate purposes to which I seek to apply it. I also further beg to be commended to the special protection of our Minister to France, and to have his active coöperation, *in procuring an audience* of the Emperor.

It has been intimated to me from certain quarters, that since the publication of my letter to the President, my appointment to a place in our French Legation would be displeasing to the French Government, and render the Legation there unpopular. *Unpopular!* All this I utterly deride and deny. Ministerial peculation is not popular in France, and its just exposure not unpopular. I assert that it will be quite as agreeable to the Emperor as to myself that we should meet without delay and settle our long pending negotiation; for he lately told me so himself, and had not Mr. Fould quickly driven me from France, we should have done so. That the Legation should be *unpopular with Mr. Fould*, however, is inevitable. As also that he and his emissaries should industriously disseminate the notion (using the Emperor's name for it, too,) that His Majesty and the Ministry closely sympathize with him; or, in other words, that they are his accomplices! But it requires little knowledge of the world to see through such transparent artifices. They can impose on no one *who does not wish to be imposed upon*. In like manner, some years ago, he filled our Legation at Paris with doubts and derision at my expense, by asserting "that they had sent an Exploration to Africa and found no gold." My patient response (as I awaited the Official Reports to the contrary) was, "Yes! they have sent to the Pacific Ocean and found no water!" These Official Reports have now arrived, and, as the result of my demonstrations to the Emperor, show, that the French are coining over one hundred millions of dollars *in gold*, per annum! In the face of such facts, there is no power in this or in any other government that can contrive to hide and baffle the plain justice of my cause.

So long as the manifest interests of the Emperor rendered secresy proper, I observed a guarded discretion even amidst the most formidable persecutions; and even endeavored to screen from scandal Mr. Fould himself, but now that the Official Reports of the Empire proclaim the triumph of my scheme, and the alarming hostilities of Mr. Fould are still going on, I esteem it full time that my voice should be heard. Justice would not desire to suffocate it. It shall be my own care that Injustice does not.

In conclusion, let me beg, that if, under the accumulated wrongs of years, occasional expressions of impatience should escape me, no portion of their import, either here or elsewhere, should be ascribed to a want of that genuine respect for your Excellency, with which now, and at all times,

I have the honor to remain with great consideration, your obedient servant,

ROBERT A. PARRISH, Jr.,
No. 1305 Arch Street.

To His Excellency, Hon. HOWELL COBB,
Secretary of the Treasury, Washington, D. C.

Finding appeals to the integrity and patriotism of Mr. Buchanan a mere waste of breath, the Claimant arraigned the French Emperor before the grand jury of the world, through the instrumentality of the following article in the newspapers.

Like a bomb in a magazine—it blew up the French Ministry, and even the Imperial family itself. The Empress eloped to Scotland, and was forbidden thereafter to sit in Imperial council. Not a franc, however, of this indebtedness was ever paid to the Claimant.

[*From the New York Herald of September* 29, 1860.]

GOLD AND CONQUEST.

Colossal Enterprizes of Louis Napoleon in Africa, &c.

Public attention has been recently attracted to the collossal operations of Louis Napoleon in Africa, by the publication of certain correspondence between Mr. R. A. Parrish, Jr., of Philadelphia, and the President of the United States. The object of that correspondence is the acquisition of diplomatic protection by Mr. Parrish, in order that he may, safely and unembarrassed, prosecute a claim upon the French Government for 15,000,000 of francs, which is the remuneration alleged to have been promised him by the Emperor for a demonstration of the Auriferous Regions lately conquered and annexed to the Empire.

The gigantic achievements of the French upon that continent, the unprecedented sums of gold which they have thrown, and are still throwing, into general circulation, and the new fiscal and political interests which are thus springing up, independently of all other considerations, render this subject one of primary importance. Believing, therefore, that a narrative of the facts would be appreciated by the banking and commercial population of your city, the following, from an acquaintance with this subject since its inception, as well as from an inspection of the correspondence of Mr. Parrish with the governments both of the United States and France, is respectfully submitted:—

When California arose in 1848, like a splendid apparition on the shores of the Pacific, an entirely new aspect was given to the geology of gold; and, for the first time, the world was prepared to reason accurately upon enlarged plans for its acquisition. That in many localities it could possibly exist as abundantly diffused as iron, was until then universally discredited. The uninterrupted and increasing product of the Uralian washings for upwards of a century had been insufficient to enlighten even the learned world on that subject. In evidence of this assertion it will curiously appear that Lieutenant Wilkes, in his Exploring Expedition—[Philadelphia, 1845, vol. V]—although his corps of savants had traversed the gold fields of California on their longest diameter just before their development, had actually encamped at Sutter's Fort, where the golden marvel was afterwards disclosed, and for some time had been sleeping on beds of gold every night—never dreamed of the opulent reality. Indeed, so far did the reality transcend even scientific suspicion or surmise, that whatever this expedition may have seen, the text of this report has not a syllable about gold.

In like manner, Sir Roderick Murchison, in his report on the Russian gold fields, undertaken at the instance of the Czar, says:—"Count Keyserling also assures me that the discovery of Mr. Hoffman relates to an area larger than France, every part of which seems to be more or less auriferous. * * * If this diffusion of gold * * be really found to hold good over so vast an area it imparts a new and most important element to our reasoning. * * * Well, therefore, may political economists now beg for knowledge at the hands of the physical geographer and geologist, and learn from them the secret on which the public faith of empires may depend."—[Geol. of Russia: London and Paris, quarto edition, 1845, vol. I, p. 648.]

If these scholars, who stood in the very highest rank of modern geologists, notwithstanding their personal explorations in the field, were not only skeptical as to the profuse existence of gold (as it is now known), but if even Sir Roderick, when alluding to the probable value of the gold fields of Hindostan and South Carolina, was silent or unadvised as to those which Mr. Parrish has since brought to light, it would imply a most mendacious intellectual coxcombry in persons ignorant of geology to affect (without the light of study or of demonstration) any such antecedent knowledge. Indeed, so utterly unbelieving was the general as well as the learned world on this subject, that although Count Strzelecki had, as early as 1838, prospected the gold fields of Australia and published the result; and although Sir Roderick, on his return from Russia, had, in 1847, endorsed these views in a public lecture, which was reported in the papers, and although he even urged the British Ministry by letters to investigate the subject, yet no action ensued from these invaluable revelations.

Such, then, was the state of universal skepticism, even until some time after the discovery of gold in Australia in 1852—a discovery like that of California, which was wholly the offspring of fortuitous circumstances, having been aided neither by learned theories, by governmental authority, nor by ministerial wisdom.

The dominant truths established by this inauguration of the modern age of gold gave a new significancy to the indications of gold already known to exist elsewhere. Then it was, and not until then, that geologists were competent to trace and demonstrate (solely from their general reading) the remaining auriferous formations of the world. But yet it does not appear that any other person than Mr. Parrish has actually attempted it. Commencing his researches in 1848, so assiduously did he address himself to the task, that in the course of two or three years, without traveling beyond the great libraries of Europe and America, he discovered and demonstrated four new gold fields of enormous national value, his geological telescope (like that of Le Verrier) detecting its object by calculation only. Two of them (those of the Kong Mountains and those of Hayti) have already become the objects of national pursuit and acquisition, for which their possessor is solely indebted to Mr. Parrish's instrumentality. The other two, which are the subject of negotiations with other governments, are not mentioned here, for obvious reasons.

A knowledge of those in St. Domingo was obtained from him surreptitiously by his Excellency Mr. Fould, Minister of the French Imperial Household, and has been pursued (without any promise or compensation to him) by the French Government.* Mr. Parrish was in Paris, amongst other visits, during

---

*A knowledge of two additional gold fields was also pilfered from the books and papers of the Claimant by the spies of Mr. Fould—one at the head waters of the Amazon; and the other in Cochin-China—both of which the French Government have seized.

a part of 1856 and 1857, when his trunks, books and papers were subjected to continual invasion and espionage by the emissaries of his Excellency, and in this way the important truth transpired. His appeals for protection against these outrages to the Commissary of his arondissement, to the Prefect of Police, to the American Minister, and to the French Minister of the Marine, were alike entirely disregarded.

Immediately upon this discovery by the French of the mineral value of St. Domingo, the best map of that island ever published, (namely, that by Piquet, Geographe du Roi et de Mgr. le Duc d'Orleans,) was reprinted with a haste so ludicrous, that whilst the date of its imprint was altered from 1840 to 1857, it still purported to have been issued in 1857 by "the geographer of the King and of the Duke of Orleans." General Santana, in reply to Mr. Parrish's inquiry for maps of the island (for the use of his company hereafter mentioned), informed him that the French Government had just issued these new editions, by some understanding or arrangement with the General. The following articles also (all of which tell their own story) then successively appeared in the Moniteur, the official journal of the French Government:

On the 24th of May, 1857, there is a notice of a submarine telegraph intended to connect this island with the French Antilles.

On the 17th of November, 1857, it is stated that a number of emigrants recently left France for St. Domingo, and a new departure is announced to their projected establishments.

On the 21st of February, 1858, an Imperial Decree establishes a line of steamships to Hayti, &c., and appropriates 1,900,000 francs per annum for its support.

On the 17th of June, 1860, the Haytien loan is announced as having been distributed at the Hotel de Ville, at Paris, under the supervision of the Minister of the Interior.

During the years 1857 and 1858, Mr. Parrish organized a company in New York for the development of these West Indian gold fields, whose plan was to connect the island with New York by steamships; to introduce steamboats on the rivers Yaqui and Yuna; to construct railways in the Vega Real, &c., and to procure from the local government general mining privileges throughout the island. In the same year he visited and prospected these formations, procured both ores and nuggets, and only reached the city of St. Domingo in time to ascertain that Mr. Reybaud, the French Consul General, had obtained from the Dictator Santana the identical grant (expressed almost in ipsissimis verbis) with that which he himself had gone to obtain. It will be found published in extenso in the Gaceta Oficial of that city, April 19, 1859. Similar concessions were also obtained by Mr. Reybaud from Hayti.

A knowledge of these encroachments by the French were promptly brought by Mr. Parrish to the notice of his government by letters to General Cass of the 18th and 24th of May, 1858, in the course of which he remarks:

"The nautical ascendancy over the larger Antilles conferred upon this island by its incomparable bays, and by its windward position; by its marked supremacy of soil, climate and productions; by its vast area and close proximity to 'the States,' gives it a political value, whether for good or for evil, far too momentous to be regarded with indifference. Nearer in time to New York than Buffalo was thirty years ago, more necessary to our expanding commerce than any other portion of the West Indies, and gaining daily and hourly in the general appreciation of the world, the time would seem to have totally elapsed when, with any prudence or safety, it can be longer abandoned to the intrigues of European governments."

These suggestions elicited no notice, and the operations of the French went steadily on. Their policy, however, might long ago have been anticipated by the perusal of a couple of editorials in your paper of the 5th and 9th of July, 1858, which announced the existence of an entente cordiale between Mr. Buchanan and Louis Napoleon, having for its object the appropriation and division of the Antilles:—France to take San Domingo, and the United States Cuba, &c.—a project still in force, but on our part not yet successfully consummated.

Hence the "Thirty Million Bill," for the purchase of Cuba, urged upon Congress by the Presidential message of the succeeding winter; the late overthrow of the Haytien Empire in the west and the Spanish Republic in the east of San Domingo (both the result of French intrigue); the resuscitation of the old Haytien debt to France of 150,000,000 francs (indemnity for the revolutionary confiscations of 1793); the concordat between the Pope (Louis Napoleon's Prime Minister) and the churches of the island, and many other indications that Geffrard and Santana are mere creatures of the French Government. In short, the French power is actually consolidated at our doors. This entente cordiale, however profitable it may have proved to certain persons, is certainly the most fatal, the most ignorant, and (since treaties not ratified by the Senate are unlawful) may even be termed the most treasonable error of diplomacy which has thus far occurred in our limited history. St. Domingo is but another California. In fact, it is risking nothing to say, that if the people of the United States had been aware of its inestimable value, and of its history during the past four years, they would have frustrated the policy of France, even at the peril of a war.

But enough of this episode.

Probably led by the alluring example of Russia (as above

mentioned,) the French Government in 1841 also sent out a commission to examine and report upon the value of the gold fields reputed to exist in Bambouk, which was a little negro kingdom in the Kong Mountains of Africa, at the head waters of the Gambia and the Senegal. As long ago as 1801 Golberry had published a work entitled, "Travels in Africa," treating, amongst other things, of this region, and giving a pretty good summary of its exploration by various travelers. So antediluvian, however, were his geological views that (Chap. XII) he estimated its annual auriferous, together with its commercial products, at perhaps $80,000, and (Chap. XI) recommended his government not to undertake its acquisition. As may be assumed, it had absolutely no effect in the development of the mines. It is certain, however, that he and all the other authorities up to 1841 were diligently considered by the French Government, before they ventured to embark in even the petty expenses of the commission of that date. The official report of that commission, by Mr. Rey, its chief, who actually prospected its gold fields, is to be found scattered through the Moniteur from 1846 to 1853, and also in the Revue Coloniale, &c., &c., together with the later explorations by Raffenel, in 1843. Rey says, as to the abundance of its gold: "It is true that in a short time its mines could be exhausted.' [Revue Coloniale, January, 1854, p. 58,] and recommends his government not to undertake "its conquest"—language which indicates that Bambouk was not at that time considered as an integral part of the colonies of France.

So manifest is this, indeed, that in the City Directory of Paris, for 1853 (originally published by the government, and bearing upon its title page the name of his Excellency M. Fould,) the colony of Senegal was defined to be "an inconsiderable post at the mouth of the river of that name." A new edition of this Directory (since issued without his name and antedated) essentially modifies this definition by terming it "a colony more or less considerable, on both banks of the Senegal." The unparalleled display of industry which thus seeks to give an artificial aspect to the neglected but easily established history of this region is worthy of admiration, and has a meaning which will be expounded in the sequel.

The voluminous report of Mr. Rey was a signal for the abandonment of similar enterprises in that direction. With the exception of numerous treaties negotiated by the Prince de Joinville and others at Bassam, Assinoa, Dahomey, &c., along the Atlantic coast, directed at commercial objects only, and not at gold (as they had invariably been), France, absorbed in revolutions up to the time of Mr. Parrish's arrival, scarcely looked beyond the confines of Algeria in any of her African speculations.

The project of Mr. Parrish for the development of the gold fields of Africa was embodied in a Memorial, now in the hands of the French Emperor. It was originally submitted to his own government in March, 1853, pursuant to a preliminary conversation with a Cabinet Officer.

From a default of means and of constitutional authority, as well as from their inability to pursue the scheme with secresy, the government, after a few weeks' consideration, declined the proposition, whereupon the Memorial and correspondence were returned at his request, not however without the emphatic commentary that—

"All the world has known that there is gold in Africa, but this is the first time that the idea of its acquisition has ever assumed a practical shape."

Another Cabinet officer, transported by its gorgeous pictures of mineral and commercial opulence, remarked:—"That in the inevitable effect of its developments upon general commerce and finance there is nothing since the discovery of America by Columbus that can be compared to it,"—an observation, as will appear in the sequel, which has been even more than realized. Had the government coöperated with him the Memorialist would have added on private account to the proposed expedition a thousand additional men.

Failing in government aid, a private enterprise was attempted with the coöperation of several gentlemen. The Messrs. Aspinwall, of New York, a large steam shipping house, were sounded as to their willingness to put on a line of steamers to the new El Dorado, which (from motives of policy) was represented as lying on the Orinoco, but already overpowered with business and anxious for repose they declined. The idea of a private enterprise was soon after abandoned. America not seeming to offer a sufficient field, Mr. Parrish proceeded to Europe, in the hope that some one of its governments might have the sagacity to perceive its value, and undertake the prosecution of his scheme; for be it parenthetically remarked—save by a few persons qualified to comprehend such subjects, his views were generally denounced as altogether preposterous, visionary and chimerical. He was even derisively asked, "If there were gold in Africa, would the world have waited for him to point it out?"—forgetting that the world had waited for Mr. Marshall in California, and for Mr. Hargreaves in Australia, neither of whom made any pretences to geological learning.

He arrived in Paris on the 16th October, 1853, and addressed himself to his Excellency M. Fould, Minister of the Imperial Household, to know if the Emperor would entertain a proposition of this nature, saying that he was prepared to demonstrate its value and its convenient accessibility to the arms of

France, provided he could secure those interests in the enterprise which he desired to retain. His Excellency responded that it would be necessary to see the Emperor, who was then at Compiègne, and that he would give a response in a few days. At the same time his Excellency was reminded by Mr. Parrish that he would treat with the Emperor only, and that his Majesty should not be put to the pains of an extraordinary audience unless prepared to prosecute the enterprise, and to make Mr. Parrish some proposals to which he could accede. No intimation was given then, or at any time afterward, that France contemplated any project of the kind, or that any of her colonies were even supposed to be rich in gold. On the contrary, the scheme was hailed with enthusiasm, and its novelty was admitted to be equal to its intrinsic importance. In a few days Mr. Parrish was informed that the Emperor would undertake it and would be pleased to see him. Whereupon an extraordinary audience was appointed for its consideration at St. Cloud, 30th October, 1853. Meanwhile (as detailed in his letter to the President, published in the Philadelphia Evening Bulletin of August 24, 1860,) his Excellency M. Fould insisted on Mr. Parrish's reception of fifteen millions of francs from the Emperor, one-third of which was to be allotted to his Excellency. This appropriation of one-third of the fruits of the scheme was not objected to, but many reasons which cannot here be entered into rendered Mr. Parrish very repugnant to the mention of so large a sum. He was told that if it was worth one franc it was worth fifteen millions; that with the coöperation of his Excellency and the Emperor, he possessed that of the whole government, &c., &c. In short, he was obliged to acquiesce, and under this necessity saw his Majesty at the time appointed. This was precisely two weeks after his arrival in Paris—a promptitude contrasting harshly with the seven years which have now elapsed since the surrender of his scheme, without the manifestation of any disposition on the part of the French government to carry out its engagements with him.

On the occasion of this audience with the Emperor at St. Cloud the conversation was in English. The Emperor stated that he had understood from M. Fould the nature of the subject, &c., and inquired if a remuneration of fifteen millions of francs would be satisfactory, or half the product of the mines for a term of years. To the latter proposition Mr. Parrish demurred, mainly on the ground of its magnitude, but otherwise intimated his consent. The subject was then discussed for some time, in the course of which he designated Africa as the scene of the enterprise, particularized some of the points where gold was most abundant, and responded to the interrogatories of the Emperor respecting the distances, the requisite expeditionary force, &c. He was then requested to lay the written evidences of the subject before the Minister of the French Marine, who should be instructed to give him a Traité, to guarantee the conditions thus agreed upon, one of which expressly provided that the money should be payable as soon as the French arms should be established in token of sovereignty over any portion of the territory indicated.

The tenor of Mr. Parrish's Memorial (which is still in the hands of the French Emperor) was substantially as follows:— To plant a missionary settlement, with one gun, upon a rocky island in the Niger below the mouth of the Tchadda, and thereby, through this, its natural outlet, to command the commerce of its immeasurable valley—a valley stretching from the Kong Mountains on the west to the remote highlands on the east, which divide the waters of the Niger from the waters of the Nile. Furthermore, by treaty or purchase, to displace the European settlements on the west coast north of the line; and thus, with the desert as a northern boundary, the Atlantic on the west, the Mountains of the Moon on the south, and western ridges of the Nile upon the far east, to establish a colony, which for its inexhaustible natural productions, and particularly for its wealth in gold, can have no rival upon the surface of the earth. Space will not admit of enlarging here upon the evidence adduced to show the facility with which these measures might be carried out, nor in demonstration of the unexampled prodigality of the gold deposits scattered for a thousand miles throughout the Kong Mountains.

The growing hostility to the slave trade of the principal Christian States was indicated (amongst others) as a means of displacing the flags of Europe upon the Atlantic coast by simply undertaking to stop the exportation of slaves north of the Equator, an engagement easy of accomplishment, as the slaves would find their best market in the mines. The southern coast of that continent might be left to the enterprising philanthropy of other Powers, &c.

On the 1st of November, 1853, this Memorial, with some of the further evidence which belonged to it, was submitted by Mr. Parrish to the Minister of the French Marine, with the understanding that his Excellency would, in a short time, decide upon the solidity of the enterprise, and in the event of his approval proceed to draw up the Traité. On the 5th of December, 1853, Mr. Parrish again saw his Excellency, who then informed him that the project had been adopted by the Emperor, that an expedition was then fitting out for its prosecution, and that the Traité would probably be ready in a few days, the delay which had already occurred being chargeable to the incessant demands upon his time by the details of the enterprise, &c. Because, a day or two after this, Mr. Parrish hesitated to adopt a creature of Mr. Fould's to be named as his copartner in that instrument, it was never delivered to him. His access to all the offices of the government was immediately cut off, and a system of vindictive persecutions directed against him which three several times compelled him to leave the country. His communication with the Emperor by letter or otherwise was defeated, and until the present time, notwithstanding the triumphant success of the enterprise, and the very considerable expense and trouble he has undergone, his interests have made no progress. The other particulars of this negotiation will be hereafter given, with his correspondence with the government of France, which is too voluminous for the present communication.

An expeditionary force of thirteen vessels and twenty-five hundred men was dispatched to Senegal (the base of operations) during December, 1853, and in the same month there commenced a series of Imperial Decrees, now amounting to two or three hundred, and for the most part published in the Moniteur, which were passed in the development of the scheme. The first, which is for the enlistment of native blacks in the colonial service of Senegal, was published on the 5th of December, 1853. Another, chartering the Bank of Senegal, on the 22d of the same month. At this date St. Louis contained thirty-nine tradesmen, and this bank, which was utterly superfluous to them, was designed as a place of deposit for the gold then in confident expectation. On the 8th of May, 1854, a voluminous decree was published, reconstructing the colonial system of France, and placing Senegal under the special presidency of the Emperor. On the 30th of May, 27th of June, and 10th of July, will be found official reports of the successful progress of the expedition. On the 10th of August, 1854, a decree appoints the officers of the Bank of Senegal. On the 13th of August, a decree establishes a corps of *gardes des mines*. On the 19th, another organizes the judiciary of Senegal. On the 15th of October the judges are appointed to the Colonial Courts. On the 23d of January, 1855, a decree establishes civil commissariats. On the 15th of March, 8th of August, 10th of October, and in several subsequent instances, decrees organize emigration companies for the transportation of "apprentices" to the Antilles, which are nothing more nor less than the native prisoners of war, captured by this expedition, beyond the numbers which were necessary for the mines. On the 3d of July, 1855, there is further legislation respecting the school of mines. On the 2d of September, 1855, is an official report of the consolidation of the French power in the upper country of Senegal. On the 22d of November there is an official report by the Governor of Senegal of the cession of territory to the French by native princes, the construction of forts, &c. On the 22d of January, 1856, there is an official announcement that treaties have been concluded with various European governments regulating the sale of arms to natives on the African coast—a decree which has an obvious significancy. On the 16th February, 1856, there is a decree constituting Oualo a province of France, &c., &c. On the 11th May, 4th July, 18th November and 31st December, 1856, are sham reports from the Governor of Senegal, intended, like many others of the same stamp, to lead inquiry away from the facts. On the 3d December, 1856, a decree effects further important modifications in the French colonial system. On the 9th April, 1857, is a report of the expedition of Mr. Flize, who bears the portentous title of Director of the External Affairs of Senegal. On the 11th and 17th April, 1857, are official announcements of treaties with England, whereby the British flag is obliterated along a large portion of the west coast of Africa. On the 30th April, 11th May, 6th July, 9th July, 11th August, 6th, 7th and 13th September, 13th and 17th October, and 17th December, 1857, will be found further reports of the continuous expansion of the French power in Africa. On the 10th January, 1858, is an official report admitting, for the first time, that the French Government is in the receipt of gold from these mines, which is here rated at 60,000 francs, but which will be shown hereafter to have been flowing into France during the four previous years at the rate of about 550,000,000 francs per annum. On the 28th October, 1858, a new ministry appears to have been created, entitled the Ministry of Algeria and the Colonies, of which Prince Napoleon was appointed the incumbent, whose report avows the consolidation of the French power throughout the auriferous kingdom of Bambouk; whilst, on the 26th March, 1859, is another decree formally erecting this ministry, and appointing as its head Count Prosper de Chasse-Loup Laubat. On the 9th February, 1860, a decree puts the African mails under a separate and special service— a decree which, on the part of those who deem it strange that all these proceedings should not have been previously known— merits specific consideration, particularly when it is remembered, that although unpublished, the decree had been virtually in force for six years, and that all the labor of the expedition was that of slaves, necessarily ignorant of the French language. On the 8th July, 1860, a decree opens the Custom House of Southern Algeria to the free admission of the commerce of Soudan, and the report of the Colonial Minister speaks of "the vast horizons then opening to France." On the 31st of the same month a land office is established by Imperial decree, and the Colonial Minister alludes to the vast and populous regions placed at their disposition, and compares them to the unpeopled territories of the United States. Commencing, also with the arrival of the above-mentioned expedition in Africa, in 1854, will be found in the same paper a multiplicity of decrees (over fifty in number) dispensing medals and decorations for military services in Senegal. In addition to this it may be remarked, that Abyssinia has lately sunk under the protection of France. French military expeditions, both from Algeria and Senegal, have in the past few years penetrated to the heart of Africa, and those who read her official journals must be perfectly aware that her designs on that continent have latterly assumed gigantic proportions. The fate of Egypt consequent upon the late Syrian complications, and that of Morocco upon those of the late Spanish war, are more than dubious. But if the world should be startled at an early day, by the arrival of new maps of Africa, dressed exclusively in French colors, from the Mediterranean to the Equator, and from the Atlantic to the Indian Ocean, let not their surprise be imputed as a fault to any omission on the part of the correspondents of the Herald. Ten years ago the sibylline leaves of the "Memorial," above alluded to, plainly foreshadowed these results as demonstrable possibilities. To-day they are maturing realities.

But apart from the revolutions, political and geographical, which this vast provincial empire is working out upon the continent of Africa, its financial developments are still more extraordinary. Indeed they transcend all that is to be found in previous history.

The gold coinage of the United States, which only once before 1834 attained the sum of a million of dollars, namely, in 1820, will be found from that date until its receipts from California—save the exceptional year 1847, during which $17,000,000 of Mexican gold coin, acquired during the war, was sent to the mint—to present a growing but moderate increment in its amount. This increment bore a more or less steady ratio with the foreign trade. That of France and England will be found subject to the same conditions. At length the mints of the United States and England felt the effects of the California and Australian mines; not, however, until two or three years after their respective discoveries. But in these effects the French mints can be scarcely said to have participated with equal promptitude. The late coinage of these several governments is as follows:

ANNUAL GOLD COINAGE OF

	England.	United States.	France.
1844,	$17,819,745	5,428,230 00	Yearly average. $2,500,000
1845,	21,223,040	3,756,447 50	
1846,	21,654,555	4,034,177 50	
1847,	25,742,500	20,221,385 00	
1848,	12,259,995	3,775,512 50	
1849,	10,889,775	9,007,761 50	

ANNUAL GOLD COINAGE OF

	England.	United States.	France.
1850, . . .	7,459,180	31,981,738 50	*17,038,478
1851, . . .	22,002,055	62,614,492 50	*53,941,914
1852, . . .	43,711,350	56,846,187 50	5,405,654
1853, . . .	59,761,955	55,213,906 94	62,592,804
1854, . . .	20,760,915	52,094,595 47	105,305,640
1855, . . .	45,043,315	41,166,557 93	89,485,564
1856, . . .	30,010,570	58,936,893 41	101,656,399
1857, . . .	24,299,300	48,437,964 00	114,512,245

This preternatural activity of the French mint was, in 1850 and 1851, due to political causes, and consisted merely of the recoinage of her own currency, in order to obliterate its antecedent and offensive political effigies, as every traveler who was much in France at that period must have remarked. The alleged coinage of 1853 in this table is a fiction. The normal coinage of the year could not possibly have exceeded $26,000,000, and $36,000,000 of the sum allotted to it should be divided amongst the three ensuing years; for it was not until August, 1854, that the auriferous flood-gates of Africa were opened and first poured their deluge into the treasury of France. The year 1852, moreover, was the period when the mints of the United States and of England (and *a fortiori* of France) first felt the combined influx from the great Eastern and Western gold fields, and if France got but a part of their gold before that date, she certainly did not get it all afterwards. Yet we find her in 1854 coining, ostensibly, from these sources, 526,528,200 francs of gold, or a sum actually surpassing the gross product of both. But as the mints of the United States and England still went on at their previous rates, we must absolutely resort to some new source of supply for a solution of this inundation. "In no other countries," says Mr. Chevalier, "does the coinage of gold attain these proportions, or anything like them." And as the total mass of gold in existence, derived from all sources, up to 1848, is estimated at $2,000,000,000, he shows that at present rates France alone, in ten years, will supply in gold coin one-half of that amount, which is the aggregate supply of the New World from its discovery up to the development of California.—[Chevalier on Gold, New York, &c., 1859, pp. 55, &c.]

To state the impossible feats of the French mint in a still clearer light, it will appear from the statistical returns that

---

*Recoinage, &c.

the average annual product of gold from 1854 to 1857, both inclusive, was as follows:

From Australia,	$46,108,273
From California,	47,249,442
Conjointly,	$93,357,725
All other sources, except Russia,	1,380,000
Total,	$94,737,715
Average gold coinage of France (same period)	102,789,962

Inasmuch as Russia retains all her own gold she is excluded from this computation, and accordingly, as there has not since 1848 been a forty-fold expansion of the commerce of France—which alone would comport with the achievements of her mint—the conclusion is irresistible that a new and indefinite supply of gold has been opened to her, in the nature of a government monopoly. In evidence of this it will be observed that the report of Mr. Magne, Minister of the French Finance, in the Moniteur of January 25, 1860, not only says "that in nine months only of 1858 the imports of gold exceeded the exports by 376,000,000 francs," but that he has otherwise been rioting in an affluence almost fabulous for its magnitude. For instance, he suddenly has 197,000,000 francs in the government chest, 200,000,000 in the treasury, 20,000,000 in the dotation to the sinking fund, a reserve of 364,000,000 in the Bank of France, and, in superaddition to all this, has paid the vast expenses of two wars, liquidated 140,000,000 treasury bonds, and (under threats of its payment) diminished the interest on hundreds of millions of the national debt from four to two and a-half per cent! Moreover, we behold that officer, in a country with mortgaged resources and colossal debts, which has been wading through revolutions for three-quarters of a century, sitting down to calculate the rates of the approaching fall in the value of gold, and to demand of economists how much of it the several nations of the earth can possibly absorb before they reach the point of "saturation." Even the most obtuse observer must have noticed that amidst the financial convulsions of 1857, which shook the four quarters of the world, the Bank of France alone stood as firmly as a pyramid. This was not the result either of conjurations or of commerce. It was the simple consequence of the Memorial of Mr. Parrish, who, notwithstanding the great benefits he has thus conferred on France, has not yet received any requital at the hands of the Emperor. Whether this has been due to political necessities, arising through a temporary fear of foreign intervention, and dictating to France the profoundest secrecy in the prosecution of her purposes, it may be difficult to say; but certain it is that she has thrown an almost impenetrable veil over all her legislative and official acts in this connection. Nor was this altogether in vain, for at one most critical period of her proceedings she stood for a time upon the very brink of defeat.* But whatever the truth, it nevertheless seems to imply a melancholy reflection upon the morality of the age, and especially upon that of the Ministries of France and of the United States, that such signal services, attended by such unexampled benefits, should still leave their author to complain that he is the victim of injustice darkened by ingratitude.

On Christmas day, 1853, the last detachment of the Naval and Military Expedition, organized for that purpose on receipt of the Claimant's Memorial, sailed from Toulon, to seize upon this much coveted territory. [Vide Moniteur, 28th Dec., 1853.]

The success of this movement soon led (as will be shown) to a Treaty with Great Britian, whereby nearly the whole English title to West Africa, north of the Equator, was, in 1857, irrevocably ceded to France, when forthwith the residue of the *extensive region pointed out in the Memorial was overrun and conquered, and is now incorporated with the French Empire.* [Vide Moniteur of April 11th and 17th, 1857.]

In the pages of the same Journal is the following report, amongst many, of the progress of the Expedition. It comprised over thirteen vessels, and some two thousand men.

French Official Admissions of the Execution of the Claimant's Proposition— Working of the Gold Mines, &c.

Report of the Governor of Senegal.

Moniteur, May 30, 1854.—Pursuant to orders from the Emperor the Minister of the Marine charged the Governor of Senegal with an Expedition destined to accomplish the reëstablishment of Pohdor, one of the Forts of the old African Company. This was to insure the free navigation of the Senegal to Bakel and beyond; and to constitute a base for *new combinations called for by the colony, &c.* * * * The territory of Pohdor is situated about sixty leagues above our establishment at St. Louis. [The mouth of the river. Attention is invited to the limited state of the colony at this time, as here officially confessed.] The Governor, Capt. Protet, *at the close of last year*, (1853) in returning from France to Senegal was provided with military reinforcements, with a supplementary flotilla, and

---
*Vide last paragraphs of Mackey's Affidavit, p. 56.

with supplies both from Brest and Toulon. Pursuant to these preparations the Governor organized at St. Louis an Expeditionary Force, composed as follows:
750 men (8 companies) of Marines.
150 men (1½ companies) of Artillery.
1 section of Artisans.
70 horsemen from the Squadron of Spahis.
25 soldiers of the Engineers.
150 Marines.
500 Black Volunteers of Senegal.

The vessels attached to the Expedition were the steamers Epervier, Anacreon, Galibi, Marabout, Ebrié, and the Serpent; the gunboat Tactique, the transports Pintade, Pilot, Ile of Oleron, and the horseboat Basilic; also, some large Shallops and various Transports hired at St. Louis. [See also Moniteur of 2d Sept., 1855, and 9th, 11th and 17th April, 1857, et passim.]

In the Bulletin of the Geographical Society of Paris, Fifth Series, Vol. I, for 1861, it is stated, "That Governor Faidherbe, after having inaugurated a *new policy*, and secured peace no longer *purchased by numberless periodical payments* to the natives, and after making the French name feared and respected by its glorious combats, is no longer *contented with a mere local influence on the banks of the Senegal*, but extends that *influence*, together with our intercourse, over spaces of *immense extent*."— [Page 5.]

In the colonial newspaper, the Moniteur du Senegal, for 1856, Col. Faidherbe, (who is already Governor of the colony) in his official report of the mode of administration of the gold mines says, that *ten officers*, whom he names, *are the only whites admitted*, the rest of the work is done by the natives. Blockhouses and barracks, constructed at Toulon, and exported in pieces, are put up on the ground. [Vide Revue des Deux Mondes, 1858, Vol. XVII, p. 861.]

And further, when alluding to the vast basin of the Niger and to Timbuctoo, he adds, "This theatre, *an extent of thirty-five or forty thousand square leagues*, peopled by millions of inhabitants, and offering an outlet for forty or fifty millions of merchandize, is a temptation worthy of a high and intelligent ambition." [Ibid. p. 877.]

"Negotiations were resumed with the Chiefs of Bambouk for the establishments, both commercial and military, of the French. The Minister of the Marine coöperating with the Minister of War, designated Mr. Maritz captain of engineers for the direction of the enterprise. The construction ... of two forts was ordered, one at Kanieba and the other at Jamba Yaya, at the head of steam navigation on the Falémé. The first intended to protect the working of the mines, the other the depot for receipt and shipment of the product. The administrative force comprises, besides the Director and Sub-director, a mining engineer, two guards of the engineers, two colonial surgeons, a commissary of marine, and two corporals of the engineer corps—10 persons in all. During the July floods, Mr. Faidherbe and Capt. Maritz initiated the assumption and possession in the name of France of the territory of Kanieba in the basin of the Falémé, twelve hundred miles in the interior of Africa!! [Ibid. page 861.]

In reserving the gold mines of Bambouk as a government monopoly, the administration has only yielded to various considerations of order. First, to improve the Colonial Budget of Senegal, whose receipts do not exceed 2,000,000f. ($400,000); of which only 250,000f. ($50,000) proceed from local sources.... Besides, in the delicate situation of our relations with Bambouk, perhaps prudence would admit of no other alternative. We shall thus arrive, moreover, at more exact notions of the actual value of these auriferous territories, whose details are altogether vague...... This gold product is diffused in the interior amongst a host of Pagan and Mussulman States, reaching the West Coast from St. Louis, all the way to Sierra Leone, and through the interior to Segou, Djenné and Timbuctoo, the three capitals of Central and Western Soudan. The mines of Bambouk, from every appearance, are only detached veins of those vast mountainous masses set down on the maps as the Kong Mountains, which divide the upper basins of the Senegal, the Gambia and the Niger, from which point as a centre of upheaval, they throw their spurs eastward to the heart of Soudan, and southward along the coast of the Atlantic. This vast upheaval is very probably a gold field, if we are to judge from the inexhaustible quantity of gold with which during the last few centuries the blacks have supplied the Europeans, without other manipulations than the crudest washings. [Ibid. pp. 860-1.]

Already for the distance of two hundred leagues into the interior of Western Africa the horrible custom of massacreing prisoners has disappeared, since the useful employment of gathering Gum and Arachides has been discovered—a striking testimony to that alliance between commerce and civilization of which, it may be hoped, that the mines of Bambouk may supply a new illustration. [Ibid. p. 863.]

In 1856 the commerce of St. Louis amounted to 11,206,179 francs. [Ibid. p. 865.]

Navigation follows the progress of commerce. In 1856 it employed 590 ships, amounting to 49,997 tons, manned by 4492 persons. Of these outside vessels 139 were French and 40 colonial; 393 were employed in the navigation of the river, and 18 foreign vessels brought coal for the use of the government, the only exception [as to the admission of any foreign craft] allowed by the rigorous rules which govern this colony. Ibid. p. 866.

After this hurried sketch it is impossible to doubt the vast career of Senegal. But the French policy must extend itself far beyond. Whilst the entire basin of the river [Senegal] must be the horizon of our immediate action, that of the Niger is opening to our influence. ... In short this double current of progress, both external and internal, must lead us to Central Africa—to the very heart of Soudan. Such is the natural destiny, or rather the horoscope of our colony of Senegal, which must be confirmed by future developments. [Ibid. 870.]

Bambouk, a rolling country, little known, is largely uncultivated—as the abundance of gold has damaged its agricultural interests. ... its extraction is so easy. [Ibid. 872.]

We may search in vain amongst the colonial domains of France for a province whose future opens with such prophetic brilliancy. Algiers alone or perhaps Guiana may be even compared with it as worthy rivals. [Ibid. 879.]

Our last military station. more advanced than that of the Romans, is at Tougourt. .... To this point we have imitated, but beyond we surpass them, by dotting the way through the Desert and its oases with artesian wells. Our most advanced station is the well at Bardad, on the route to Ourgla, the first commissary station to Timbuctoo. When hereafter these oases shall be united by a forest of palms, as the result of the fountains which Desvaux is boring everywhere—then a railway will connect Biskra with Tougourt, &c. ... Civilization will penetrate the Desert, streaming on one side toward Egypt, and the other toward Senegal. ... England advancing from the Cape and France from Senegal will clasp hands in the centre of Africa. [Ibid. Vol. LII, p. 637.]

The reëstablishment of Fort Pohdor, sixty-five leagues from Saint Louis, was the first object of the campaign. This Fort was constructed in the last century by one of the African Companies, to protect the commerce which extended from the factory called the Cock as far as Bakel. The population of Foutah, which it overawed, profiting by the commotion caused by the Revolution of 1789, destroyed it toward the close of that century. Under the new French occupation under the Bourbons, *and up to 1834,* the military defence of the river, *between St. Louis and Galam,* was limited to the armed Posts of Richard Toll and Dagana, thirty-five to forty leagues above the capital. From this last point *to Bakel, a distance of seventy leagues, everything was uprooted.* ..... The expeditionary column left St. Louis in transports on the 28th of March, 1854, and in a few days arrived at Pohdor. The natives were dispersed. Masters of the ground, the engineers completed a fort in the space of forty days. The immediate result was the suppression of the customary taxes exacted of traders..... Building lots, instead of being given away, have been sold at auction since 1857. [Ibid. Vol. V, 1858, p. 529.]

The territory of Oualo was ravaged so as to leave neither asylum nor resources to the Trarzas.* [Ibid. p. 530.] At the end of six months the whole interior of this province was subjugated..... To confirm this success, the Post of Dagana, on the river side on the frontiers of Oualo and Foutah-Dimar, was reconstructed, fortified and armed. [Ibid. p. 531.]

The government is constructing at Toulon a steamer of very light draft to navigate the affluents of the Senegal and head waters of the Niger...... Public opinion, until now, has remained either estranged or indifferent to all questions relative to our simultaneous possession of Algeria and Senegal. [Bull. Soc. Geog., Vol. XVII, page 379.]

European civilization is advancing into Western Africa. France has taken possession of the Territory of Dakkar, opposite to Gorée. [Ibid. 1857, p. 490.]

Africa now is in a great measure a dependency, first, of France and England, and secondly, (although in a very limited degree) of Portugal. Egypt is developing mainly under the influence of France. All the Berber territories, thanks to Algeria, are under our sway. Senegambia is much more French than English, &c. England alone strives to countervail our supremacy in the North of Africa by her continual aggrandizements in the South. Southern Africa is already, for the most part, morally and materially a dependency of the British Flag. [Ibid. 1866, p. 38.]

Opinions of French Philosophers and Statesmen respecting the Value of the Claimant's Proposition to the Emperor.

In the Bulletin for 1855, of the Geographical Society of Paris, the views of the Count d'Escayrac de Lauture are given in the like strong confirmation of those originally contained in the Claimant's Memorial, viz: "Soudan, a region ignored by antiquity, but equal nevertheless to Brazil or to India, and much more near to us, is now especially engrossing the attention of scholars, and equally deserving of the consideration of statesmen." Vol. X, p. 89. [Vide Memorial, ante p. 12.]

Mr. Pellegrini (introduced by its President,) delivers an address to this same learned society in 1857, and says, "I will restrict myself by telling you that the realization of this project [the development of commerce between Algeria and Central Africa] will be *the most philanthropic work of the age*, the most advantageous to commerce and to agriculture, in short *a fruitful source of opulence to France.*" [Ibid. Vol. XIII, p. 194.]

---
*Hence the slaves shipped to the West Indies as apprentices.

Mr. Laroche de Clermont-ferrand, to the same society, says in 1859, "I desire to refer to the Explorations made to connect our two colonies of Algeria and Senegal, via Timbuctou. It is unnecessary to speak here of *its immense utility and vast consequences.*" [Ibid, Vol. XVII, p. 375.]

In the same sense Elie de Beaumont, Senator of France, and President of the Geographical Society, in his address to the General Assembly of the Society, Dec. 16, 1859, says, "I am convinced of the utility of a direct connection between Algeria and our colony of Senegal, *now so happily expanded* under the sage enterprises of Col. Faidherbe, &c. . . . This will unite the countries *we already possess* with those lately traversed by Dr. Barth." [Ibid, Vol. XVIII, p. 303.]

The Vice President of this society, Mr. Jomard, in 1860, delivering his annual address, remarks: "The industry and the genius of Europe will, ere long, penetrate into these distant regions, [Central Africa] and there introduce arts, civilization, *and perhaps better governments.* Navigation will establish itself on those interior seas, whose banks will become explored, the vegetable and mineral riches of the African soil will be recognized and studied, and will be exchanged with the products of the rest of the world. This universal commerce will cause Africa to participate in the growing progress of civilized countries." [Ibid, Vol. XIX, p. 344.]

In Vol. XIX is a communication from Governor Faidherbe to Mr. Jomard, saying (1860): "Our acquaintance with Senegambia is constantly augmenting, through officers whom I am daily dispatching in all directions." [p. 512.] In Vol. XI, he further says: "Nearly the whole of the rivers descending from this range of mountains [the mountains of Kong] wash down gold," [p. 282.] and that "the study of Africa is in a manner to study *the very future of France itself!!!*" [p. 25.]

In Vol. XVII, ibid, is a scientific communication commenting upon the ethnography, the physiology, the anatomy, the maladies, &c., &c., of Central Africa, subscribed by a Mr. Peney, who wears the significant title of "Surgeon-in-Chief of the French Army of Soudan!" [p. 321.]

On the 25th June, 1860, an Imperial Decree opens the Custom Houses of Southern Algeria to the free admission of the commerce of Soudan; in other words, Soudan is a recognized part of the French Empire. On the 31st of the same month, by another Imperial Decree, an African Department of Public Lands is created, and the Colonial Minister, who succeeded Prince Napoleon in that office, alludes in his report "to the vast and populous regions placed at their disposition," and compares them "to the unpeopled territories of the United States."

In the Moniteur of Sept. 22d, 1860, is a speech of the Emperor to the Algerines, delivered during his late visit to Africa, in which he utters the exulting pride with which the expanding power of France on that continent is contemplated by him. He says: "To extract from this soil all those treasures deposited there by Providence—and which a bad government would leave unproductive—*such is our mission. We will not fail in it!* ..... In pursuing this object, let us hope that other emigrants will follow the example which has been set, and that new communities will come to establish themselves upon this soil—*now and forever French!*"

As early as the 8th of May, 1854, a voluminous Imperial Decree was published in the Moniteur, reconstructing the entire colonial system of France, detaching Senegal, however, from the system, and placing it under *the immediate Presidency of the Emperor.* [Post p. 100]

To-day that colony of Senegal, which in 1853 had a little worthless trade in Ground Nuts and Gum Arabic, no inland Forts nor "free navigation" of the river sixty leagues from the coast, and contained a population of twenty-nine white men, glitters with growing magnificence under the immediate Presidency of the Emperor, and extends its flag over thirty-five thousand square leagues of territory, a region as large as continental Europe. In the New American Encyclopedia, published in 1866, it is now described thus: "Senegal; a French colony, on the west coast of Africa, consisting of several Forts along the *whole course* of the Senegal and Falémé Rivers, &c., &c. The French have been gradually extending their power in this region for several years past, and *subduing the surrounding tribes.* The trade is chiefly in gold, ivory, wax, gum, &c. The establishment is under a Colonial Governor, and has five companies of native sharp-shooters, a Marine Battery, a detachment of Sappers, and a squadron of French and Native Spahis, besides a body of Militia and TWELVE VESSELS OF WAR."—[Vol. XIV, pp. 505, 506.]

To these manifestations of growth and power it may be added that the colony has now a newspaper, (the Moniteur du Senegal,) a Bank, a local Ministry—one of whom wears the portentous title of "Director of the Exterior Affairs of Senegal"—[vide the Moniteur, April 9, 1857,] a corps of civil officers surpassing in number the entire number of white men in 1853, a Judiciary, a Post-office Department, and a Chief of the Bambouk Gold Mines at Kenieba!!—[See the Almanach Imperial, 1859, pp. 890, &c.]

Here then at length the mask is dropped, and the Claimant's letter of Havre, July 4, 1854, in response to that of Mr. Fould, and the foreshadowings of his Memorial are verified to the letter.

Commencing in 1854, immediately after the conquest of Bambouk the French mints for many consecutive years coined, as we have seen, over five hundred millions (500,000,000) of francs in gold, per annum, which demonstrably could have been derived from no other source. A list of some hundred Imperial Decrees also have appeared in the Moniteur, the official journal of the Empire, promulgated by the Emperor, in his diligent prosecution and development of the Claimant's Proposition. Meanwhile the Claimant has received neither the promised Treaty nor any payment whatsoever from the Emperor or Government of France; and all his efforts and sacrifices in this connection, running through many of the best years of his life, have been fruitlessly thrown away. The inhuman persecutions, moreover, he has suffered in this connection surpass the belief of the uninitiated. He has been virtually enchained by the Emperor—like Prometheus to the rock—whilst those Hebrew harpies have been feeding on his vitals.

If, instead of receiving, he was striving to pay to the Emperor this same amount of money, it is not probable that Mr. Fould and his emissaries would have invented so many fictitious reasons for barring access to His Majesty. At all events, by a singular Nemesis the Emperor has lost more by this prohibition than the Claimant himself. The Claimant can still give a value to his African Proposition of more moment to France than many times the amount of his Claim, and if permitted would have gratuitously revealed to the Emperor a new and separate mass of information, more tributary to the permanent interests of his dynasty than all the resources of Africa.

IMPERIAL DECREES,

And Articles in the Moniteur—the Official Journal of the French Empire—Published by Order of the Emperor, Relating to his Development of the Auriferous Territories of Africa, revealed to him by Mr. Parrish.

1853, Dec. 5. Decree. Recruiting of native blacks authorized.
   16. Steamer Laborieux dispatched to Senegal.
   22. Decree. The Bank of Senegal established!
   28. The frigates Armide, Constitution and Montezuma dispatched to Senegal with troops and provisions.
   30. Decree. Grain free of duty at Senegal.

1854. Mar. 10. Return of steamer Montezuma.
May 6. Medical Corps of the Navy reörganized.
8. Decree. A Colonial Board established, and the entire colonial system of France reörganized. Special provisions respecting Senegal!!
8. Decree. Naval officers to reside out of port.
8. Medical Naval Corps further reörganized.
12. Decree. Medical Officers to reside out of port.
30. Official Report of the Military Expedition of fifteen vessels and twenty-five hundred men, moving up the Senegal toward the gold fields. Conquest of Pohdor.
June 27. Official Report of the Expedition, Conquest of Djalmath, and movement against Dimar.
July 3. Decree. Regulating compulsory labor. [In the mines!]
10. Decree. Respecting vessels south of 30° N.
10. Official Report of Faidherbe, Commander of the African Expedition for conquests in Africa.
11. Imperial distribution of Medals for military services in Africa.
16. Decree. Extraordinary appropriation to the Department of the French Marine of 16,667,000 francs, equal to 15,000,000 in gold being the amount due to Mr. Parrish.
Aug. 10. Decree. Mr. Rey appointed Director of the Bank of Senegal.
13. Decree. Regulating admissions to the Corps of "Guards of the Mines."
19. Decree. Reconstruction of the Judiciary at Senegal.
Oct. 12. Decree. Tariff on Breadstuffs from Senegal.
15. Decree. Appointment of Judges to the Courts of Senegal.
Nov. 9. Decree. Regulating the administration at Goree, in Senegambia.
9. Imperial distribution of honors for military services in Africa.
1855, Jan. 7. Decree. Regulating candidates for the Corps of "Guards of the Mines."
9. Decree. Regulating foreign vessels entering Goree.
23. Decree. Establishment of a civil Commissary Department on the route to the interior of Africa from Senegal.
23. Appointments in the civil Commissary Service.
25. " " " "
Feb. 5. Decree. A civil Commissary Department also

established in Algeria. [Expeditions from Algeria and Senegal penetrate Africa, and meet at Timbuctoo on the Niger.]
1855, Feb. 9. Decree. Intestate Laws established for the colonies.
  28. Decree. Compulsory labor regulated in the colonies. [Not slavery, of course.]
Mar. 4. Decree. Regulating compulsory labor in the colonies.
  13. Compulsory labor extended to Senegal.
  14. Decree. Tariff on provisions to Senegal.
  15. Decree. Organizing emigration companies, with power to transport Africans to the West Indies, &c., under the name of Apprentices!!
May 2. Decree. Iron houses admitted duty free at Senegal.
  7. Decree. Regulating appointments to the Colonial Board:
June 17. Decree. Commissaries of the Marine appointed for the Colonies.
July 3. Decree. Regulating a School of Mines.
  8. Official Reports of further conquests by the African Expedition.
  27. Imperial distribution of medals, &c., for military services in Africa.
Aug. 8. Decree. Regulating emigration companies, empowered to transport native blacks to the West Indies, &c., under the name of Apprentices.
  24. Decree. Regulating the administration of justice in the colonies.
  25. Decree. Regulating administration of justice in the colonies.
  25. Official Report. The Bank of Senegal commences its functions!! [A depot for gold.]
Sept. 1. Decree. Regulating the Securities of Emigration Companies.
  2. Official Report of the Governor of Senegal, announcing the triumphant establishment of the French power *through the whole country of the Upper Senegal;* a general pacification, &c.
  13. Official Report of the Colonial Banks.
  14. " " " "
Oct. 10. Decree. Regulating emigration companies.
  21. Official Report of the Minister of the Marine.
Nov. 22. Official Report of the Governor of Senegal, of the continued extension of French authority in Africa, through the regions indicated to the Emperor by Mr. Parrish.

1855, Nov. 24. Decree. Appointments in the Colonial Commissary Department in Africa.
Dec. 21. Decree. Regulating the Security given by Emigration Companies.
30. Decree. Regulating the Colonial Post Offices!
1856, Jan. 22. Treaties, regulating traffic in arms on the West Coast of Africa, with various Governments of Europe!
26. Decree. Nominations in the civil service at Senegal. Heads of Departments!!
31. Decree. Nomination of Naval Commander on the West Coast of Africa.
Feb. 16. Decree. Oualo, in Senegal, established as a French Province, and Senegal divided into four circles.
May 11. Official Report of the Governor of Senegal; further extension of French power.
July 4. Official Report of the Governor of Senegal; further extension of French power in Africa. Pillage of the Moors near the river Senegal.
Nov. 18. Official Report of Governor of Senegal; further extension of the French power in Africa.
Dec, 3. Modifications of the colonial system.
31. Official Report. Further extension of the French power in Africa.
1857, Jan. 12. Official Report. Further extension of the French power in Africa, in the Gold Regions.
Mar. 18. Decree. Relating to transportation of native blacks, under the name of Apprentices.
28. Official Report of Governor of Senegal. A Ferry for caravans from the interior established at Pohdor, on the river Senegal.
31. Decree. Establishment of a French College at Algiers for instruction in Arabic—150 free pupils.
April 9. Official Report from Senegal by Mr. Flize, Director of the "Exterior Affairs of Senegal," of vast extensions of the French power in the auriferous territories of Africa, particularly throughout the kingdom of Bambouk.
11. Official Report of the Treaty between France and England concerning the obliteration of the English Flag along the west coast of Africa, as expressly indicated to the Emperor by the Memorial of Mr. Parrish!!!
17. Official Report of Treaty with England respecting the west coast of Africa.
28. Decree. Regulating Emigration Companies.

1857, April 30. Official Report from Senegal; final surrender of the Moors of the Sahara to the French authority.
May 10. Cultivation of Indigo proposed in Upper Senegal.
11. Official Report from Senegal. Boundaries of Galam admitted as alleged by the Claimant.
June 5. Decree. Establishing a Court for Mussulmans at Senegal. Appointment of a Cadi, &c.
13. Decree. Authority to Emigration Companies withdrawn.
15. Decree. Regulating the School of Mines.
July 6. Official Report from Senegal. Razzia against the Moors.
9. Official Report from Senegal. Further razzia against the Moors.
25. Reports from Medina, Africa.
Aug. 11. Official Report of further razzia against the Moors.
Sept. 6. Official Report of same.
7. " "
13. Official Report from Fort Medina, on the Upper Senegal.
Oct. 9. Decree. Nominations in the Courts of Senegal.
10. Decree. Tariff on Grain at Senegal.
13. Official Report of Governor of Senegal. Further conquests and pacifications on the Upper Senegal.
17. Official Report from Senegal. The French power finally consolidated throughout Senoudebou, Bambouk, Bondou and Kaarta, being part of the territories indicated to the Emperor by the Memorial of Mr. Parrish.
18. Decree. Nominations to the Courts of Senegal.
21. Decree. Improvement of the Harbor at St. Louis, Senegal.
25. Decree. Imperial Medals for military services by natives of Senegal.
Nov. 8. Decree. Regulating "Emigration" Companies.
Dec. 11. Decree. Authorizing exportation of native blacks under the name of "Emigrants."
17. Official Report respecting Fort at Bakel, on the Upper Senegal.
1858, Jan. 2. Decree. Conditions of admission to the school of "Guards of Mines."
10. Official Report from Senegal. Navigation of the River Senegal. River commerce, 1,200,000 francs. In *gold, 60,000*.

1858, Jan. 11. Official Report from the Upper Senegal. The whole country submissive.
25. Decree. Nominations to the Judiciary of Senegal.
April 18. Decree. Authorizing the recruiting of native blacks as sharp-shooters of Senegal.
25. Official Report of a razzia against "Ndiambour" in Cayor, Senegal, with a French force of 2500 men.
29. Decree. Awarding medals for military services in Senegal.
May 1. Official Report of conquests over native Moors through the Desert of Sahara; the boring of Artesian wells, and the cultivation of artificial oases.
2. Official Report. Extensive recruiting of blacks at Senegal.
5. Decree. Nominations and promotions in the army for military services in Senegal.
7. Official Report respecting commerce with Central Africa across the Desert.
8. Official Report of a Military Expedition into the Desert from Algiers.
Aug. 25. Official Report from Senegal. Final subjugation of the Moors on the left bank of the river.
Oct. 18. Official Report from Senegal. A large military force in Bambouk celebrates the anniversary of its cession to France, on the 15th August, 1858. The French Government admitted to be engaged in mining gold!!!
23. Official Report respecting the Gold and Platinum in Bambouk.
28. Official Report of Prince Napoleon, Minister of the Colonies, announcing the establishment of French authority over vast districts in Africa, indicated to the Emperor by Mr. Parrish.
1859, Jan. 1. Decree. Distributing medals for military services in Senegal.
14. Official Report. Commerce in Senegal flourishing.
18. Nomination of French Naval Commander for West Coast of Africa.
20. Decree. Establishing and endowing Bishopricks and Archbishopricks for the Colonies.
20. Decree. Naval command on the West Coast of Africa extended to the Gaboon.
27. Decree. All the West Coast of Africa, as far as Sierra Leone, placed under the central authority of the French Colony at Senegal.

1859, Mar. 17. Decree. Establishing a Steam Towing Company for the harbor of St. Louis, Senegal.
  26. Decree. Appointing Count Prosper de Chasse-Loup Laubat, Minister pro tem. for the Colonies, vice Prince Napoleon.
  28. Decree. Promotions and honors for military services in Senegal.
May 2. Decree. Nominations at Senegal.
  17. Official Report of a Treaty between the Colonial Governor of Senegal and the native King of Toro.
Sept. 5. Official Report of Governor Faidherbe, respecting the trade of Arguin and western part of the Desert.
  11. Decree. Promotions and honors for military services in Senegal.
  19. Official Report of Fleet dispatched to construct a Fort at Saldé.
  29. Decree. Duty on Grain at Senegal.
  30. Official Report of razzia against the Moors.
Oct. 27. Official Report. Submission of native Chiefs to the Governor of Senegal.
Nov. 1. Official Report from the Gold Mines.
  14. Official Report of Mr. Berg, one of the Sub-Directors of the Mines of Bambouk.
1860, Jan. 1. Decree. Medals awarded for military services in Senegal.
  1. Decree. Regulating Tariff on Grain at Senegal.
  12. Decree. Regulating Mussulman Courts in the French Colonies.
  25. Official Report of Mr. Magne, French Imperial Minister of Finance, disclosing the infinite opulence of the French Government, and that over one hundred millions of dollars in gold per annum had been coined in the French mints for many years!!!
Feb. 9. Decree. African Mails to be kept under special control.
  17. Decree. Telegraph established between St. Louis and Goree, Senegal.
  27. Official Reports of the commerce and further conquests in Senegal, and of gold in the Bank of France.
March 9. Official Report on the Gold Mines of Kenieba, Senegal.
April 11. Decree. A corps of native African "Mechanical Engineers" added to the army of Senegal.
  27. Decrees. Nominations in the Courts of Senegal.

1860, June 4. Official Report of the commerce of Kano, great central mart of Soudan.
July 8. Decree. Free trade authorized between Algeria and Soudan, which the Colonial Minister, Chasse-Loup Laubat, reports as comprehending "vast horizons."
31. Official Report of Colonial Minister that France has secured "vast territories like those of the United States, but occupied by a people which France wishes neither to pillage nor expel." A public land office established.
Aug. 7. Official Report of journey to Tagaat, an Oasis northeast of St. Louis, Senegal.
25. Decree. Regulating a Towing Company at St. Louis, Senegal.
31. Accounts of the Oases of the Sahara.
Sept. 14. " " "
22. Official Report of the Emperor's Address in Algiers.
30. Decree. A Grand Cross of the Legion of Honor granted to Chasse-Loup Laubat, Minister of the Colonies.
Oct. 1. Decree. Establishing Hospitals in Algiers. Official Report of Minister of Colonies.
12. Official Report of Journey in Algiers, &c.
22. Decree. Distributing from two to three hundred Medals for military services in Africa; also Honors.
24. Decree. Distributing Honors to natives.
25. " " " "
Nov. 3. Decree. Promotions for military service in Africa.
10. Decree. Colonial Credit Company established.
10. Official Report of Minister of Colonies.
12. Decree. Algerian R.R. chartered.
15. Decree. Nominations to civil and military offices in Africa.
16. Decree. Nominations to civil and military offices in Africa.
17. Official Report of the assassination of Mohammed El Halid, King of the Trarzas, *for entering into a Treaty* with the Gov'r. of Senegal.
18. Official Report of fifty Artesian wells being dug in the Desert of Sahara, by the French in opening highways across it.

Soon after the above-cited article appeared in the New York Herald of September 19, 1860, and a letter from the Claimant was delivered to Count Persigny, then Ambassador to London, the newspapers reported—the retirement of Mr. Fould from the Ministry, the absconding of the Empress incognito to Scotland, the arrest of Mirés (Chief of the celebrated Credit Mobilier), for frauds of unprecedented magnitude, the Emperor's threat to arrest the Count de Morny for "speculation in mines," and the prohibition of the Empress (by Imperial Decree) from sitting in Council during the absence of the Emperor as theretofore!!!

The Claimant interprets these events thus:—The charges against Mr. Mirés were for swindling, breach of trust, and forgery.

Some unauthorized person must have assumed the character of a partner of the Claimant—(which could only have been accomplished by the perpetration of the three crimes in question and the connivance of Mr. Fould,) and then, instead of accepting in settlement the fifteen millions of francs, (as the Claimant's letter, p. 25, to Mr. Ducos preferred,) insisted on the other alternative of "half the product of the mines." This would promptly have realized the sum of $120,000,000, (which was the amount of the Mirés frauds,) and would account for the liberal bribes diffused amongst the Imperial Family, the Ambassadors of the United States, &c. That Mr. Fould actually connived at all this, is manifest by his audacious letter to the Claimant of 27th June, 1854, (p. 34,) in which he impudently refers to such a co-partner. well knowing the utter groundlessness of the allegation.

It was also reported by the newspapers, that the whole Imperial family, the Empress inclusive, had accepted bribes from Mirés, ranging in amount from five hundred thousand to five millions of francs. Even the wealthy Princess Demidoff the sister, and old Prince Jerome, uncle of the Emperor, united in thrusting their larcenous fingers into the pockets of the Claimant and dividing the pillage with the Jews who had planned this villainy. The following Decrees then appeared, viz

1860, Nov. 24. Decree. Count Walewski is appointed Minister of the Imperial Houschould in place of Achille Fould, resigned.
   25. Decree. Reconstructing the Ministry. Abolishing the Ministry of Algeria and the Colonies;

also abolishing the Ministry of the Imperial Household. Modifying the Forms of Procedure in Parliament; and appointing Marshal Pelissier Governor-General of Algeria!!!
1860, Nov. 27. Decree. Appointing a new Ministry: Mr. Persigny to the Interior; and reconstructing the Government of Algeria.
Dec. 1. Arretè (of 24th Nov.) Mr. Jules de Saux appointed Chief of Bureau to Minister of State.
5. Decree. Marshal Vaillant appointed Minister of the Imperial Household until the affairs of the office are wound up and closed.
11. Decree. Further modifying the Government of Algeria.
21. Decree. Reconstructing the entire Ministry and making new appointments.

In addition to this voluminous catalogue of Decrees, nearly an equal number have since been promulgated by the Emperor, in his active prosecution and development of the Claimant's Proposition. But their further quotation is certainly superfluous. If these do not suffice to demonstrate that Napoleon III has nefariously "seized and pocketed" the interests of the Claimant, there is no accumulation of testimony which could possibly establish that proposition.

Letter from Mr. Parrish to Mr. Cass, U. S. Secretary of State.

PHILADELPHIA, 10 April, 1860.

SIR:—On the 2d day of December, 1858, I sent your Excellency, for record in the Department of State, a copy of my correspondence with the Government of France, touching my claim for fifteen millions of francs upon that government; my desire being that the claim should be comprehended in the list, called for by the resolution of the Senate, of June 14th of that year.

In my letter enclosing this correspondence, I defined the claim in the following words, to wit:

"The claim is based upon the Emperor's Parole, which was pledged to me in consideration of certain evidence demonstrating the existence of a gold field similar to that of California, and accessible to the arms of France, which I had the distinguished honor of bringing to his notice. It was to become payable as soon as the authority of France was established in any part of the territory indicated. This condition has been long since fulfilled, and the French Government is actually employed in working the gold mines."

I have now to complain that when the list was received and printed by the Senate this claim was erroneously stated to be: "In fulfillment of a verbal agreement entered into by *Mr. Fould, Minister of Finance, and confirmed by* the Emperor, to pay the Claimant 15,000,000 francs, upon his demonstration of the existence of a gold field," &c. As appears by Senate Ex. Doc., No. 18, of the XXXVth Congress, Second Session, page 16:—which error works a material injury to my interests in the premises: First, because it is at variance with the truth. Second, because it transfers the responsibility for this debt from the Emperor (upon whose honor alone it rests) to an alleged Minister of Finance; and, Third, because standing thus, it appears to bear the authority of my sanction.

This sanction, I beg leave to say, it never had, as I never so much as saw or communicated with the French Imperial Minister of Finance, at any time, or on any subject! Inasmuch, therefore, as such a mistake, if uncontradicted, would greatly multiply impediments to an ultimate liquidation of the claim, I entreat that proper measures may be taken to thoroughly rectify the same upon the records of the Department.

If any official communications from the French Government have been made to the Government of the United States in relation to me, or to my claim, I further respectfully request that I may be furnished with copies of them.

I have the honor to be, with great consideration, Your Excellency's obedient servant,

R. A. PARRISH, Jr.

To His Excellency LEWIS CASS,
    Secretary of State, Washington, D. C.

Reply.

DEPARMENT OF STATE, }
WASHINGTON, April 12, 1860. }

ROBERT A. PARRISH, Esq.,
    Philadelphia.

SIR: I have to acknowledge the receipt of your letter of the 10th instant, relative to your claim against the French Government, and to state in reply that nothing has been received from it on the subject.

I am, sir, your obedient servant,
JAMES APPLETON,
Assistant Secretary

Mr. Parrish to Mr. Seward, U. S. Secretary of State.

PHILADELPHIA, November 3d, 1865.

SIR:—The written letter, the four affidavits and the printed letters which accompany this, will supply the evidence of a claim upon the French Government (amounting to Fifteen

Millions of Francs) which has long been due to me, and which by order of the French Emperor was to have been embodied in the form of a written contract or Traité, but of which latter, as well as of the money itself, I have been most wrongfully defrauded. The details of this fraud will more fully appear, from my correspondence with the French Government, which, together with a list of some two or three hundred Imperial Decrees passed by that Government in the prosecution of its engagements with me, is on file in the Department of State.

This claim is for an amount personally promised to me by the Emperor himself, without whose promise I refused to surrender the consideration upon which it is based, as was distinctly understood and assented to by Mr. Achille Fould, Minister of the Imperial Household, prior to the audience at which that promise was made.

After the reiterated delays and persecutions to which I have been exposed in this matter, it is proper that your Excellency's attention should be aroused to a clear perception of the facts of the case; and that the outrageous and insulting prevarications of which I have been the victim, should not be allowed to pervert your Excellency's sense of duty, or to silence my cry for justice.

Your consideration, therefore, of the following points is respectfully invited:

First. That the integrity of this claim, precisely as alleged by me, has never been denied by any officer of the French Government, but on the contrary has been distinctly admitted:

Second. That the consideration for which the Emperor promised me this money has been fully and confessedly realized by him, as appears by announcements in the Moniteur (the official journal of the French Government) of September 2d and November 22d, 1855, December 31st, 1856, January 12th, and October 17th, 1857, January 10th, 18th and 23d, 1858, &c., &c., &c.:

Third. That the money for my payment was appropriated by an Imperial Decree in July, 1854, but was embezzled by a party fraudulently introduced into the negotiation as my copartner, without my knowledge or consent, through the instrumentality and coöperation of his Excellency, Mr. Achille Fould, then and now Minister of the Imperial Household:

Fourth. That Mr. John Y. Mason, late Minister of the United States to France, and James Buchanan, late President of the United States, actuated by impure motives, and yet knowing the entire justice of my claim, so far from heeding my appeals for justice, added insults and affronts of their own to those I had received from officials of the French Government, and exerted the influence of their great offices to defeat and discourage my efforts for the settlement of this claim:

Fifth. That in the face of this, one of the most stupendous of recorded frauds, the allegations of my wrong-doers are entitled to no weight and can be respected by those only who seek my injury.

Sixth. That the printed synopsis of my claim, in Senate Ex. Doc., No. 18, of the XXXVth Congress, Second Session, page 16, is a fraudulent corruption of the synopsis filed by me in writing at the time: said fraud having been perpetrated by an emissary of Mr. Fould's, through certain persons, whom I can name, if desired, and was intended to screen the Imperial honor from that glaring infamy which a truthful state of the record would have disclosed:

Seventh. That no charge of a failure of consideration, and no charge of payment or of a release by me, in whole or in part of said claim, has ever been made or can be made; but on the contrary, it is admitted that the Emperor's honor still stands committed to me for the payment thereof; wherefore, I am sure, if my own Government would simply intervene so far as to procure me an audience with him, that I could adjust said claim myself.

If it be not incompatible, therefore, with your Excellency's general policy or duty in the premises, (whilst submitting afresh for record, under your recent call, this corrected statement of my claim,) I would respectfully ask that I may be appointed an Attaché or Assistant Secretary, *without salary,* to our French Legation, and that our Minister should be instructed to procure for me another audience of the Emperor without delay.

With great consideration, I have the honor to be of your Excellency the very obedient servant,

R. A. PARRISH, Jr.,
No. 1305 Arch Street.

To his Excellency, Hon. WM. H. SEWARD,
Secretary of State, Washington, D. C.

Mr. Seward, U. S. Secretary of State, to Mr. Parrish.

DEPARTMENT OF STATE,
WASHINGTON, November 27, 1865.

ROBERT PARRISH, JR., Philadelphia.

Sir:—I have to acknowledge your letter of the third inst., enclosing papers relating to your claim on the French Government.

The papers appear to relate mainly to declarations of yourself and third persons, as to a negotiation with the Emperor of the French. What appears to be wanting, is any evidence beyond your own statements, of a promise made by the Emperor. If such a promise should be established, it will be re-

quisite to show that it proceeded from him *in his political capacity, and not as an individual,** before it can form the basis of any representation from this Government to that of France. Your obedient servant,
WILLIAM H. SEWARD.

Mr. Parrish to Mr. Seward, U. S. Secretary of State.

PHILADELPHIA, December 2, 1865.

Sir:—By Your Excellency's letter of the twenty-seventh ultimo, acknowledging mine of the third ultimo, (which letter was accompanied by affidavits, &c., &c., relating to my claim upon the French Government,) some misgiving is expressed as to whether my claim is to be understood as a claim upon the French Government, or upon the French Emperor in his private or individual capacity, and also as to the existence of any admissions of the integrity of this claim by the French Government, beyond the assertions of my own and the other affidavits.

Had Your Excellency *had leisure, amidst your multifarious duties, to have perused my correspondence* with the French Government, neither of these doubts could have arisen. That the Emperor gave me his stipulated Parole for his Government, for the payment of the sum mentioned, is spread all through that correspondence, from end to end, without qualification, and is admitted, both by himself and his Ministers, precisely as I have stated it. The admissions of an adversary are the most conclusive and the highest order of evidence acknowledged to exist under any code of laws.

With a view to an economy of the time and labors of Your Excellency, I would respectfully beg you to assign me an audience of an hour, at some convenient day, when I will abundantly satisfy you, by the record, that there is no room for candid doubt or hesitation in the premises, as to either of the points mentioned.

I can not but esteem it a peculiar misfortune, moreover, that my affidavit, well fortified as it is by the affidavits of others, and by all the well-known historical truths of the case, (particularly by that of the gold coinage of France rising from two and a half millions of dollars to one hundred and fourteen millions of dollars per annum, after the development of my scheme,) should, nevertheless, be challenged in any Bureau of my own Government, whilst it stands without a syllable of contradiction or question elsewhere, either in or out of France.

I have the honor to be, of Your Excellency, the obedient servant. R. A. PARRISH, Jr.
To His Excellency, Hon. WILLIAM H. SEWARD,
U. S. Secretary of State, Washington, D. C.

---

*Did human effrontry ever surpass this language!] the Treaty between the French Government and the Claimant being the theme of the whole correspondence!!

Mr. Seward, U. S. Secretary of State, to Mr. Parrish.

DEPARTMENT OF STATE,　}
WASHINGTON, Dec. 5, 1865.　}

R. A. PARRISH, Jr., Philadelphia.

SIR:—In reference to your letter of the 2d inst., I have to say that the legal gentleman employed in this Department in the examination of Claims, reports:

That upon perusal of the papers filed by you, Dec. 2, 1858, he finds no admission of the validity of your claim for fifteen millions of francs, nor of the terms of what you style the Parole of the Emperor of the French:

That the papers tend to establish these FACTS:

That you were engaged in a negotiation with the Emperor, the result of which was to be embodied in a Traité or written contract: that the negotiation was [so] far abortive that no written contract was ever executed, and no sketch or memorandum of it seems producible. That according to your understanding of the case the French Government has availed itself to its advantage of information furnished by you in the confidence that you would find a remuneration in the anticipated Traité, and that your efforts to appeal to its sense of honorary obligation proved unsuccessful.

It is not perceived that any oral communications can impart additional strength to your Claim; any documentary evidence you may desire to supply will be received and considered.

Your obedient servant,
WILLIAM H. SEWARD.

Mr. Parrish to Mr. Seward, U. S. Secretary of State, embodying his Argument upon Principles of the Civil and the Common Law.

PHILADELPHIA, Dec. 18, 1865.

SIR:—Your Excellency's letter of the 5th instant, whose receipt on the 6th I have the honor to acknowledge, gives an abstract of the report upon my claim on France, by the "legal gentleman" employed in your Department.

Its import is, that "upon perusal of the papers filed [by me] December 2d, 1858, he finds no admission of the validity of [my] claim for fifteen millions of francs, nor of the terms of what [I] style the Parole of the Emperor of the French."

"That the papers tend to establish the FACTS, that [I] was engaged in a negotiation with the Emperor, the result of which was to be embodied in a Traité or a written contract; that the negotiation was [so] far abortive that no written contract was ever executed, and no sketch or memorandum of it seems producible."

"That according to [my] understanding of the case, the French Government has availed itself, to its advantage, of information furnished by [me], in the confidence that [I] would find a remuneration in the anticipated Traité, and that [my] efforts to appeal to its sense of honorary obligation prove ineffectual."

With all deference I respectfully urge that this opinion is erroneous and untenable, being alike inconsistent with the very language of the correspondence, as well as with those fundamental principles, both of logic and of law, which are involved in the subject.

Indeed, knowing as I do that the emissaries of his Excellency Mr. Achille Fould visited Washington during the presidency of Mr. Buchanan, and obtained the active coöperation of that officer in abusing, at discretion, me and my interests, I am led to assume that the opinion of the "legal gentleman" in question was delivered long before your Excellency entered the Department, and at a time when a leprous and most legitimate suspicion attached to every functionary then in power. I am the more inclined to this conclusion, that this opinion is but the reiterated language of those same emissaries, as uttered to me in Paris long before. But however this may be, that "legal gentleman" (as everybody else), in determining a question of this character, must needs disregard all other considerations, and estimate its value and binding force by those accepted principles alone which regulate the jurisprudence of civilized nations. In this view of the case, I maintain, that on the contrary, conclusive "admissions" by the French Government of the integrity of my claim can be readily established by the correspondence, sufficient to estop them from any defence to it, and trust to make the same apparent in the sequel of this letter.

It may be premised, however, that the correspondence warrants no assumption, as the "legal gentleman" intimates, that "I would find a remuneration in the anticipated Traité," but quite the reverse.

Furthermore, it may be premised, that in the interpretation of this correspondence, a legal mind is authorized to construe from the acts and words of parties their intent or animus, which is a legitimate test both of their meaning and their morality. If an immoral or fraudulent purpose becomes conspicuous, every intendment of law is to be taken against the party criminated; for, by the codes both of the civil and the common law, "contra spoliatorem vel furem, omnia præsumuntur." If, therefore, the intent to defraud me sullies the face of this transaction (as the "legal gentleman" himself seems virtually to admit), then every presumption of law will be in my favor and against the French Government. Accordingly, if I were "engaged in a negotiation with the Emperor, the result of which was to be embodied in a Traité or written contract," which can be proved to have been unfairly withheld, then a case of palpable turpitude is made out against the French, which allows them no escape from accountability to me. Professor Christian, in a note to Blackstone, [Vol. 3, b. 3, c. 9, p. 139,] says: "If an agreement is by parole, but it is agreed it shall be reduced to writing, and this is prevented by the fraud of one of the parties, performance of it will be decreed. [And see Fonblanque, Tr. of Eq., b. 1, c. 3, s. 8 and 9, where the subject is fully and learnedly discussed.]"

With these prefatory observations, your Excellency's attentive scrutiny is now invited to the words and tenor of the correspondence.

Failing, after my interviews with the Minister of the French Marine—in November and December, 1853, to obtain further access, either to him or to the Emperor, (which, until they had divested me of my scheme, had been extended with alacrity) and Mr. Mason, our Ambassador, refusing to aid me in these efforts, "unless some of the Ministry should write to me," I thereupon addressed to Mr. Ducos my letter of Paris, May 29th, 1854. This was written *ostensibly* to obtain the Traité, but actually to procure if possible a written admission of my interview with the Emperor—the Emperor's promises—Mr. Ducos' reception of me, and my demonstrations pursuant thereto—together with the approval and execution of my scheme. In this effort I was successful. My letter ran as follows. [Vide p. 25.]

Now, to these inquiries and trenchant allegations, addressed to a ministerial agent of the Emperor, acting under his immediate orders in the premises, and in a weighty matter of fifteen millions of francs, his reply (if he reply at all) should be plain, direct and unequivocal. Equivocation or evasion would stamp upon the French Administration the badge of a most shameful fraud. The principles of the common law, and of common honesty, as well as those of common sense, (to say nothing of the well recognized usages of business in such matters) all unite to justify my view of the subject. That Minister well knew that the contents of my letter were either true or false, namely: that the Emperor had received me in audience, and had given me his parole as alleged, or had not; that he, the Minister, was under orders to receive and treat with me on that basis, or he was not; that I had fulfilled conditions on my part, or had not; and that the Emperor had or had not adopted my scheme, and at that identical moment had a large naval and military Expedition in Africa engaged in its prosecution.

If these statements were known to be false; if the Minister had not received me upon this basis, and at the dates thus particularly specified, and had not again and again verbally admitted the points as thus charged, is there any one (except the "legal gentleman" quoted) who could credit that the Minister would have replied to me as he did, *or would even have replied to me at all?* The inference is irresistible, that any answer of the Minister, made under such circumstances, *unaccompanied by negation,* regard being had to the enormous sum of money involved, to the delays and evasions already complained of, and to the peremptory challenges on all these points, which pervaded my letter, would amount to an absolute admission of their verity. His reply is marked, moreover, by all the characteristics of serious precision. It admits generally all my allegations, by denying none; it also admits most of them by direct assertions which are *susceptible of no other meaning.* His letter is as follows:—[Vide p. 27.]

By way of caption, this letter, it will be perceived, contains a note, giving as usual, a specific title or synopsis to its contents, and warning me that *my replies* must be marked in a corresponding manner. "My replies." If the correspondence was not expected, and *intended to go on,* and upon the identical basis of the letter just received from me, (for he suggested no other) such a note could not have been necessary, and would certainly not have been introduced. This title alone, therefore, in the absence of qualification, admits as correct the tenor of my letter, and avows it to constitute a recorded part of the current business of his Bureau. In other words, my Proposition had been adopted upon the basis of the Emperor's promise, as alleged.

He then proceeds in the text of his letter, formally to acknowledge the receipt of mine, by date, and reminds me that I ask for the "results" (suites) of my proposition, and gives them to me. In this he was in error. In point of fact I had demanded the results *of the Exploration in Africa.* I know already that my Memorial had been referred to a committee of the Academy of France; had been by them approved, and that it had been adopted and acted upon by the Government. At our last interview he himself had apprised me that he was organizing the Expedition (as the correspondence charges), that its multitudinous details had usurped the whole of his time until then, and "that his Majesty had ordered an Exploration of the region specified." The results of that Exploration, therefore, were what I anxiously sought, inasmuch as it was "upon the conquest of any portion of the territory mentioned," that the money was to be payable. He, however, gives the results, (transpiring in the previous December) of his original investigations into the merits of my proposition. He not only admits then, as it is perceived, that the proposition (as in my letter mentioned) was received, and examined, and disposed of, but he proceeds to acknowledge that his Report in relation to it—going beyond its mere adoption and approval—(for he intimates nothing of disapproval) had passed upon the expedients necessary for its immediate execution. This Report, he adds, had been dispatched to the Minister of the Imperial Household—or in other words, to the Emperor. It cannot be believed that the Minister would have elaborated and returned to the Palace a formal report upon such a proposition, and referred to that report in reply to such a letter of inquiry, and invited a further correspondence upon it, without noticing the discrepancies (if any existed) between the nature "and value" of the proposition he had reported upon, and that which was the clearly defined subject of my inquiry. His admitted completion of a working plan to carry out my scheme precluded every hypothesis of its rejection; nor has such a thing ever been intimated from any quarter. His additional admission, "that he has just written to the Minister of the Imperial Household," &c., clenches the evidence, if any were wanting, as well to sustain the general allegations of my letter, as to compromise afresh, in regard to them, the attention and plighted promise of the Emperor. Before the Emperor that report was then lying, ratified, approved, executed, and my further correspondence respecting it invited. If, then, your Excellency will refer to the decrees and official reports, promulgated by the Emperor in the prosecution of my scheme, and to the recorded movements of the Expedition, dispatched in December, 1853, to the Kong Mountains (all of which are embodied in my record in your Department), I defy the possibility of a doubt, *as to its adoption and execution by him precisely upon the terms I have alleged.*

But even this is not all. Justice required that the Minister should have been more explicit. Under such circumstances, evasion or equivocation are more than suspicious; they amount to fraud. Silence becomes crime. Upon this point the equitable principles of the common law which are derivative from and identical with those of the Civil law (the law of France) are unanimous. Kent observes: "No one who peruses (the Civil law) can well avoid the conviction that it has been the fruitful source of those comprehensive views and solid principles which have been applied to elevate and adorn the jurisprudence of modern nations." [I Com's, p. 547.]

Starkey says: "In general, an admission may be presumed, not only from the declaration of a party, *but even from his acquiescence or silence.* As for instance, when the existence of the debt, or of the particular right, *has been asserted in his presence, and he has not contradicted it.*" * * * * *

"Evidence of this class declines, by gradual shades, from the most express and solemn admissions, down to expressions and acts which afford but remote and weak presumptions as to the particular fact in question; for it has already been seen that the conduct of the party himself, who knows the truth of the fact, or *who may be presumed to know it*, is always evidence against himself." [II, Starkey on Ev., p. 26.]

The Emperor had referred me to the Minister of the Marine, as his representative, to carry out the terms of the Imperial promise, and it is therefore altogether immaterial whether it be the admissions or the silence of the Minister, or of the Emperor himself, which go to acknowledge and define the terms of that Parole. In either case the admission is equally conclusive. By the proceedings of the Minister the Emperor is irrevocably bound. On this point, also, the legal authorities are clear, unanimous, and positive. The author last quoted declares that:

"When a party refers to another for an answer on a particular subject, the answer is *original* evidence against him, since he makes the referee his accredited agent for the purpose of giving the answer." [Ibid. p. 29.]

"But it seems to be *a general rule*, that what an agent does or says within the scope of his authority is binding upon the principal, whose agent he is; so that not only an agreement made by an agent is binding upon the principal, but so are *all the declarations of the agent at the time* which in any manner affect or qualify the nature of the agreement." [Ibid. p. 30.]

I maintain, therefore, that this answer of the Minister of the French Marine, *even if it stood entirely alone*, affords irrefutable evidence of the pledge of the Emperor's Parole to me, upon the conditions I have stated. His admission is the Emperor's admission. For, I repeat, disputing nothing in my letter, he passes upon it as it stood, and invites my further correspondence upon that basis. But it does not stand alone. Other representatives of the Emperor also answered for him in the same sense, as the correspondence shows. Apart from which, still others by innumerable reports published officially, and running over the entire period of the past twelve years, admit that vast regions in Africa (specified in my proposition) have been conquered and annexed to France, and that their gold mines have been developed by that Government.

If the plea be offered that a Minister's error, oversight or fraud might still leave the Imperial honor unimpeached, however it might involve his legal liability, I cheerfully accept the plea; notwithstanding that the tenor and results of my correspondence with Mr. Ducos would seem to have been promptly made known to the Emperor. My letter, moreover, to the Emperor of the 8th of June, 1854, is traced directly to his custody. [See Col. Mackay's affidavit, forwarded to your Excellency in my last—p. 55, ante.]

The Emperor's reply (by the Duke of Bassano, his Grand Chamberlain,) confirms these views. It is as follows [vide p. 33]:

In the due course of business the subject must have been

reviewed before this last reply was given. That review would comprehend three letters received from me, one by Mr. Fould and two by Mr. Ducos, all within a few weeks and of similar tenor. It was incumbent upon the Emperor, therefore, to disavow their reiterated allegations or to stand bound by their renewed admission. He consented to stand thus bound. He could not and did not deny them, even constructively or by inuendo. Pursuant to the legal authorities above quoted, therefore, I am entitled to insist and do insist that his repeated silence or acquiescence under the circumstances *is an absolute admission of the truth of my letters*, nor can an intelligent or disinterested criticism possibly arrive at a different conclusion.

The language of this august reply is worthy of particular attention. Whilst it withholds the solicited audience, it is much more than a mere refusal, and purposely goes further. It does not simply say "that the Emperor cannot receive me," nor does he decline to receive me any further on the subject. But the words are, "he cannot receive me *just now*," (en ce moment) and "in conformity with my expressed desire," (comme vous en avez temoigné le desir.) That "expressed desire," be it remembered, was for an audience in connection with my Proposition, coupled with a mention of my previous audience in October, of the object and result of that audience, of his promises to me, of my reference to the Minister of the French Marine, &c., &c., that all this on my part had been done, that *my scheme had been adopted, an Expedition ordered, but the Traité not yet delivered to me*," &c., &c.

Now, your Excellency will, I am sure, admit that nothing but the truth of these allegations could possibly have elicited such a reply. Whilst the expression, "just now," incontestibly implies that at some future and more convenient season my "expressed desire" for another private audience shall be accorded, upon the basis stated, as my acknowledged right. Again I repeat, that if in the reserved and guarded language of these official letters, a sinister or unfair purpose appears, or even an attempt to cloak with doubts the pure integrity of the subject, under the authorities cited, every construction which they will bear must be made in my favor.

In super-addition to the foregoing, if anything further were requisite to place the justice of my claim upon impregnable ground, it is to be found in the fact that *no pretence of the denial or contradiction of my statements is to be found in the entire correspondence.* The French Government has never made and can never make any such denial!!

That the personal promise of the Emperor, as an uncompromising condition precedent to the surrender of my Proposition, should have been exacted as a security for this money, is due to the fact that France had absolutely nothing else to give. A retrospect of the predicament in which that country stood, when for the first time I was the recipient of the Emperor's *hospitality*, will justify my tenacious demand for his parole. The Empire had not yet crystallized: it was a mere name—an individual! With much more justice than Louis Quatorze, might Louis Napoleon have exclaimed, "L'Etat, c'est moi." France was a camp; Paris a fortification; the Government in a state of siege. Six hundred thousand troops were under arms in its defence against the people. The rains had scarcely washed from the Boulevards the red blood spilt in the massacre of the Coup d'Etat! I knew no augur who could tell me how long the extemporized empire would endure. Ministers, moreover, are forgetful; they make mistakes; they are often rash, reckless, and even unscrupulous. Of Monarchs not so justly can such things be predicated. They personate a dynasty—not an ephemeral interest. And, moreover, amongst the factions that were striving for mastery in France, my sympathies and my judgment were alike enlisted by the Emperor's. His was manifestly the worthiest. For these, among other reasons, I was led to put my trust in him alone; and felt assured that if I could but secure his promise, such a promise would be kept. And I still believe it. The "legal gentleman" seems to intimate, however, that notwithstanding "the fact," that I was engaged in a "negotiation with the Emperor, the result of which was to be embodied in a Traité, or written contract," that because neither a Traité, or some "sketch or memorandum of it seems producible," that no such thing as a valid claim upon that Government can exist! and this, I presume whether the Traité was withheld through fraud, accident, my absence from Paris, or other cause; and even though it may now be awaiting my return at the Ministry of the French Marine. He virtually declares that there is no value in an Emperor's Parole! I respectfully insist that in this he is in error. Indeed, having shown my correspondence to some of the most eminent lawyers in Philadelphia, they one and all agree that his opinion "is but a sorry compliment to the profession." I strongly suspect that he is the identical "legal gentleman," who, when he first perused my Memorial in 1853, furtively dispatched a *protegé* to Portugal. Whereupon that Government established a line of steamers to San Georgio del Mina (mentioned in the Memorial) and has since then derived immense wealth from the gold mines of that place, and this without any pecuniary loss, it is to be presumed, either to the "legal gentleman" himself, or his protegé.

I assert that Napoleon III could and did bind his Government as potently by giving me his Parole—(all that I stipulated for)—as I could bind myself were I to take the French tabacco now at Richmond upon a promise to pay for it.

As to the value of the consideration realized by France, there is evidence, (on file in this case in your Department,) to show that this important scheme had been previously submitted to my own Government, that it was approved by a "legal gentleman," and that its execution was abandoned here only from a destitution of authority by the President to act without the aid of Congress. The Cabinet-officer, indeed, to whom it was referred, remarked, "that all the world has known there was gold in Africa, but this is the first time that the idea of its acquisition had ever assumed a practical shape." The coinage of the French mints, immediately after the receipt of gold from Africa, (obtained in the prosecution of my scheme,) rose from an average of two and a half millions of dollars per annum, to over one hundred millions of dollars, a sum *to which no Government, either ancient or modern, has ever approximated!* It not only renders France the most opulent of Governments, but far exceeds the aggregate gold coinage of the United States and England, the unexampled productiveness of whose auriferous Territories is a matter of world-wide renown. The following figures will make this truth more apparent.

French gold coinage, from 1795 to 1854, 58 years, $339,534,455 of which a vast amount was *recoinage.*—[Vide Annuaire Stat., 1853, p. 157; 1855, p. 294.]

French gold coinage from 1854 to 1858, 4 years,	$410,961,000
United States " " " " "	200,632,000
British " " " " " "	120,114,100

In conclusion I will add that my own affidavit to this letter, as well as a separate affidavit enclosed, sets forth such a case as would enable me to cite any private citizen, either of France or of the United States, before their respective tribunals of justice. Your Excellency will, I trust, concede that the oath of a respectable citizen of the United States is quite as worthy of credence as that of any officer in the French Administration. If my allegations or affidavits were even contradicted, I might, nevertheless, assert an equal claim to credit; but remaining, as they are, entirely uncontradicted, and, as I have shown, corroborated by the French Government, I will hope that you will now feel authorized to treat my Claim as well founded, and to take the usual and necessary measures for its liquidation.

I reiterate here, that my more immediate request is for an appointment, *without salary*, to the office, either of Secretary or Attaché, to our legation at Paris, and that our Minister should be instructed to procure for me an official audience of the Emperor, so as to enable me to settle this Claim in person.

To obtain this audience my unavailing efforts have consumed the last twelve years, in the course of which I have demonstrated its utter impracticability without the aid of my own Government. If the object of this audience, instead of *receiving*, were *to pay to the Emperor* fifteen millions of francs, all the argument, and affectation, and finesse, which have beset the subject, would have disappeared. Twelve days would have been sufficient. Less time sufficed to procure my original audience! Neither embezzling Ministers on that side of the Atlantic, nor their subsidized instruments on this, would have discovered any prospect of a war (!) or other puerile barrier in my way.

Had I been a citizen of England, my claim would have been settled long ago. Your Excellency well knows how that summary government acts in similar cases. Almost her entire diplomacy has commercial objects. Her treaties relate to little else. Her Ambassadors are daily employed in the enforcement of English claims against all nations. There lives no Emperor so potent as to be able to pillage an Englishman with impunity. There is no foreign Ministry in the world that, either by silence or mendacity, can put an English claimant in the wrong, and, whilst they greedily pocket his money, can defame him infamously, lay plots for his character and his life, and impudently laugh at his demands for justice. In view of the present power and dignity of our Republic, I respectfully submit that to succumb to such indignities is for us no longer necessary. Whatever the evils of the past, a better system ought to be inaugurated. The American people will maintain and vindicate it.

I have the honor to be, of your Excellency, the obedient servant.

ROBERT A. PARRISH, Jr.,

To His Ex'y, Hon. W. H. Seward,
Department of State, Washington, D. C

Sworn to and subscribed before me, this seventeenth day of January, A. D., 1866. DAVID P. BROWN, Jr.
Commissioner.

Mr. Parrish to Mr. Seward, U. S. Secretary of State.

Philadelphia, March 15, 1866.

Sir:—Enclosed are photographic fac-similies of five letters received by me from high official personages in the French Government, touching my claim for fifteen millions of francs promised to me by the Emperor. Except Mr. Fould's first letter, they were all written after the Emperor had received the consideration for which his parole was pledged. The disingenuous, and, I might say, the unprincipled spirit of evasion which characterizes them, is deserving of note, and, taken in connection with the unexampled effrontery with which my interests were practiced upon, and the persecutions and malignant abuse of which I have been the victim, followed up, as they were, by the forgery of my papers in your own Department in 1858, (as particularized in my letter to your Excellency of December 18th ultimo, and accompanying affidavit,) a case is presented, which I am convinced your Excellency will find it impossible to extenuate.

In view of the unusual magnitude and moment of the subject in many respects (which seem to make it quite an exceptional case), I would respectfully invoke for it your personal examination.

Of the receipt of the letter and affidavit mentioned, sent through the Hon. Chas. O'Neill, your acknowledgement is respectfully invited.

With great consideration, your obedient servant,
R. A. PARRISH, Jr.

To His Exc'y, Hon. WILLIAM H. SEWARD,
Secretary of State, Washington, D. C.

Mr. Seward, U. S. Secretary of State, to Mr. Parrish.

DEPARTMENT OF STATE, }
WASHINGTON, April 17th, 1866. }

R. A. PARRISH, JR., Philadelphia.

SIR:—I have to acknowledge the receipt of your Memorial, attested on the 17th January, 1866, and two accompanying documents.

The 33d section of the Act to Regulate the Diplomatic and Consular System of the United States, approved August 18th, 1856, provides that "no Attaché" shall be allowed in any case, nor any "Secretary of Legation" otherwise than as provided in said Act.

The Ministers of the United States address foreign Sovereigns on business, only through their Ministers of Foreign Affairs, and cannot be instructed to ask for a private claimant what it would be offensive to propose for the representative of the nation.

Very respectfully, your obedient servant,
WILLIAM H. SEWARD.

Mr. Parrish to Mr. Seward, U. S. Secretary of State.

PHILADELPHIA, April 24th, 1866.

SIR:—Your Excellency's letter of the 17th instant, in reply to mine of December 18th, 1865, apprises me that my request for aid to procure a private audience of the Emperor of France cannot be granted in the manner therein proposed.

May I respectfully inquire whether there is any other way in which the same end can be accomplished, and also, whether any further testimony is deemed necessary to substantiate the validity of my claim, as a claim, for Fifteen Millions of Francs, guaranteed by the personal promise of the Emperor?

I should furthermore beg to be advised if the Government of the United States will adopt *any* measures for the settlement of my claim. The present military and murderous operations of the French Government in Mexico, (*avowedly and solely* aimed at the just enforcement of French claims there) would seem to warrant any decent and humane course which my Government deemed expedient in the premises. Moreover, the Emperor's late speech to a Deputation of the Legislative Bodies of France, dwells with such unction upon his "love of justice," that I am convinced he would be under the most profound obligations to your Excellency for giving him an easy and ample opportunity to illustrate the truthfulness of that speech in a prompt and honest settlement of my claim.

I have the honor to be your obedient servant,

R. A. PARRISH, JR.

To His Ex'y, Hon. W. H. SEWARD,
Secretary of State, Washington, D. C.

Mr. Seward, U. S. Secretary of State, to Mr. Parrish.

DEPARTMENT OF STATE,
WASHINGTON, May 11th, 1866.

R. A. PARRISH, JR., Esq., Phila.

SIR:—I have to acknowledge the receipt of your letter of the 24th ultimo, relative to your claim against the Emperor of France, and in reply to inform you that this Department cannot, under the circumstances disclosed by the previous correspondence, urge that claim. If it is well founded it is not doubted that you can *obtain justice through the employment of competent and reliable counsel at Paris;* but as you have been already informed this Government *has gone as far as courtesy and usage will warrant in its intervention,* in a case of private contract with a foreign Sovereign.

I am, sir, your obedient servant,

WILLIAM H. SEWARD.

[The Petitioner utterly denies that the Department of State ever intervened *in any way* whatsoever in the premises as insinuated. In order to dispose of the further jesuitical inuendo of this letter, the Claimant authorized two of the most influential Counsel that perhaps ever left America, to negotiate a settlement of this Claim. They brought him back nothing but falsehood.]

December, 1860, Mr. Fould retired from office, probably foreseeing a coming storm. The occasion is reported thus:

Mr. Fould, former Minister of State, is now in retirement,

having refused all posts of honor that were offered him by His Majesty. * * * * *

When Mr. Fould took his leave the following scene occurred. You are no doubt aware that Mr. Fould has ever been a warm friend and most devoted servant to Louis Napoleon, WHO, IN HIS DAYS OF ADVERSITY, HAD AT HIS DISPOSAL THE ZEAL AND COFFERS OF HIS FRIEND. At their last interview Mr. Fould said: "Sire, allow me to assure your Majesty that he will ever find in me a faithful subject and friend, and that my life and *my fortune* shall be ever yours." The Emperor rose from his seat, embraced his Minister and said—"Mr. Fould, I rejoice to know that although I lose a Minister, my old friend I still possess." [N. Y. Herald, 17th Dec. 1860.]

THE MIRÉS FRAUDS.

The Empress of France, Prince Jerome uncle of the Emperor, the Princess Mathilde his sister, Count de Morny his illegitimate brother, President of the French Senate, &c., all bribed by Mr. Mirés, the Jew. He is imprisoned for swindling, breach of trust, and forgery.

The connection of Count de Morny with financial speculations *in Mines*, and the occurrences which had taken place in connection therewith, are attracting considerable attention in Paris. Cabinet Councils had been held upon the subject, and it was thought that legislative inquiry would result. [N. Y. Herald, 11th Jan., 1861.]

The Empress Eugenie is not allowed to attend Cabinet Council as formerly. [Ibid. 12th Jan., 1861.]

Several persons connected with the transactions in mines had been arrested. [Ibid. 9th March, 1861.]

It is whispered that Mr. Mirés will make some remarkable revelations concerning the financial transactions of great personages..... Mr. Mirés was arrested at nine o'clock last night [17th Jan., 1861,] on various charges. He is in custody at Mazas. It is rumored that several persons of standing are more or less implicated in this affair, and that disclosures, as well as serious consequences to individuals, are likely to follow. It is the general topic of conversation everywhere. [Ibid. 11th March, 1861.]

The great excitement of the week has been the arrest of the celebrated financier Mirés. Some time back an ugly hitch occurred in his affairs, and his books were a few hours in the hands of the officers of justice. His son-in-law, Prince de Polignac, averted the storm at that time by seeking an interview with the Emperor, and obtaining from his Majesty an order for the release of his books. It was subsequently rumored about the city that Mirés *would not have escaped had he not been concerned with high personages;* and rumor even went so far as to state that the Emperor himself had mixed in the speculations of Monsieur Mirés. Annoyed at these scandalous reports, the Emperor determined that a stop should be put to them, and that the best method of so doing was to ventilate the business affairs of Mirés. So at a recent council of Ministers his Majesty asked M. Delangle, the Minister of Justice, whether due attention was being paid to the Mirés affair. M. Delangle answered that enough was already known to arrest that individual, but that he judged great care was needed in transacting the proceedings, as the consequences would entail ruin upon so many. The Emperor answered that the shock must not be avoided; that public morality must be satisfied. In this view his Majesty was warmly seconded by Count de Persigny. A rumor of their proceedings having come to the ears of M. Mirés, he wrote to the Emperor a letter, the contents of which *conveyed that many of his Majesty's nearest surrounders were implicated with Mirés, and that in case he was dealt with harshly he would expose all.* The Emperor at once, upon receipt of this epistle, sent for Count de Morny, M. Billault, and one or two others, and the result of the conference was the order given to the police to arrest M. Mirés. This was done the next day (Sunday) while the financier was at dinner. Again did Prince Polignac seek the Emperor to plead for his father-in-law, but in vain. His Majesty's answer was, "Let him clear himself of the charges made against him."

Great was the consternation on Monday when it became known that Mirés was in prison. Rumors, startling, and many of them unfounded, circulate, but no one can doubt that many, very many personages *of great distinction*, are deeply compromised by the papers of Mirés, now being examined by the officers of the law. We have been startled by the sudden death of M. de Richemont, collector of taxes in this city. He committed suicide. It is alleged that he was to be arrested, and got wind of the fact, and in his dismay committed the fatal act of taking his own life. Several arrests have taken place; but as all is done in the greatest secrecy it is almost impossible to say who are those now in prison.

The fall of poor Mirés is a fearful crash. The amount of the failure is currently stated at 600,000,000 francs, or $120,000,000. Rumor says three Ministers are compromised most seriously—Morny, Rouher and Magne. Gen. Fleury, too, is among the delinquents.* The Princess Demidoff—Mathilde, the sister of the Emperor, is in the vortex, a check of 500,000 francs having been given to her. [Ibid. 13th March, 1861.]

---

* A nephew of this General came to the United States and procured an introduction to the claimant, during the progress of the intrigue stated on pp. 64 and 65, ante.

The defalcations of M. Mirés—the report of which has probably already reached you—are of such absorbing interest that all other topics of discussion are neglected.

When it is remembered that this eminent financier has been mixed up in some degree *with almost every governmental transaction since the advent of the Empire;* that he is, or rather I suppose we must now say was, the proprietor of the Constitutionnel, the organ through whose columns the picked writers, the chosen statesmen and ministry of the government alternately admonished, instructed, threatened or pacified the listening ear of Europe; that he was the intimate associate of Morny, the Emperor's half brother—if being a son of his own mother, the Queen Hortense, can make him so—of Morny, who, himself though holding high office, is double dyed in speculation: when, I say, such facts are remembered, it is easy to believe that the summary consignment of M. Mirés to the prison at Mazas as a common felon is quite enough to give pause and reflection to the public mind.

Go wherever you will, nothing else is spoken of. People call to mind how the peculations of Teste and Cubieres in Louis Philippe's reign gave warning of the rottenness that lay at the foundations of the citizen monarchy. They now look around on the wondrous prosperity which clothes everything in France, and ask themselves if circumstances really justify it. *How is it, they say, that we can thus afford, not only in Paris, but in every town and hamlet of the empire, to indulge in an expenditure which electrifies with astonishment all other nations, but which we take as easily as if the gold of California and Australia were all our own? How is it that France is being converted into an earthly Paradise, that everywhere enormous works, magnificent palaces, parks, roads, meet the eye, and that our former domestic economy is gradually being converted into a profuseness and expenditure almost fabulous?*

Men but yesterday contented to toil in the simple routine of their original calling are to-day striking the stars with their lofty heads, dazzling the multitude with a display of unbounded wealth. Is not this affair of M. Mirés the first dropping out of that stone which shall show the "untempered mortar" of the whole construction?

It is well known that Mirés, finding things coming to the worst, went with Viscount de Richemont, a member of his committee in the management of his numerous railroad transactions, to Count de Morny, and declared that unless he were allowed assistance from the Bank of France his fall would be inevitable, and that with his ruin that of others must follow. Morny, it is understood, had, with his usual shrewdness, been gradually getting out of all engagements with Mirés, and took high ground. It is then said Mirés wrote a letter to a common friend, which was afterwards shown to Morny, the result of which was the instant arrest and imprisonment of M. Mirés. As for the poor *Viscount de Richemont, a dose of prussic acid has settled his accounts in this world*. I should never be surprised to hear that his jailor had a sleepy eye to any attempt at self-destruction. If, as is universally supposed, the disclosures his trial will elicit will strike at the very roots of the *imperial entourage*, it is impossible to suppose that the enormous power of the empire will not be exerted to prevent them some way or other. [Ibid. 13th March, 1861.]

The Priests are industriously circulating the rumor that the Emperor is to divorce the Empress Eugenie for her adhesion to the Pope's temporal power.*.......

The Mirés affair has done much to weaken the confidence of the provinces in the Government, it being made apparent to the people that the Emperor's *entourage* were deeply implicated in the speculations of Mr. Mirés. The mystery thrown around the whole is calculated to increase the misgivings of the people. It is justly asserted that more than ample time has now passed since the arrest of Mirés for the making of any charge that was to be made. The long silence would go to show that time is being taken to let the influential and useful persons implicated get clear. [Ibid. 3d April, 1861.]

The Emperor was determined to ascertain how far certain persons holding a high position were or were not identified in Mr. Mirés' speculations. Such persons have refunded any bonuses that may have been accorded for "services of influence," and renounced all future intercourse with Mr. Mirés' House. This fact has greatly reduced the political interest excited by the imprisonment of Mr. Mirés, who by the way is still in confinement. It is now generally believed that arrangements will be made calculated to insure the liberation of the incarcerated banker.

The storm appears to have blown over which threatened to annihilate Mr. Mocquard, the Emperor's Private Secretary. Mr. Mocquard has not himself been one of the speculators, but his son, formerly secretary to his father, has of late retired from public affairs, in order to devote himself exclusively to private affairs—in other words to devote his time to the Bourse. Now he is known to be largely implicated in Mr. Mirés' business, and for a long time it was thought impossible to conceal the apparent complicity of the father, but second thoughts are always best, and it seems now to be decided that *a greater scandal would arise from the disgrace of one so near the person of the Emperor, than from his retaining his office* UNDER A SUSPICION WHICH IS OF TOO GENERAL A CHAR-

---

* This divorce would indubitably have ensued had she not been the mother of the Prince Imperial:—not on account of the Pope, however, but of the Mirés frauds.

ACTER TO BE PARTICULARLY INVIDIOUS!!!! [Ibid. April 16, 1861.]

It is asserted that although the CHIEF OFFENDERS in the Mirés case, have been extricated from their difficulties by the Court—a few scape-goats will be sacrificed. On dit that Mr. Collet-Meygret, Receiver General of the Department of the Jura has been dismissed, and that the son of a man of high standing at Court has been politely requested to resign his lucrative post at the Ministry of Public Works. It is also currently reported that Mr. Mocquard, the Emperor's Secretary, is about to retire from public life. [Ibid. 26th March, 1861.]

Discussion in the French Senate on Mirés' Frauds.

Mr. Dupin directed attention to the recent financial scandals. Count Simeon endeavored to justify his participation in the affairs alluded to. Mr. Billault said that the Government had instituted a strict investigation. Government desired that the guilty parties should be punished. The President said that public morality imposed upon Senators the duty of guarding against becoming engaged in such affairs. Prince Napoleon said: *not only the Senators but also the high functionaries of the Government.* [Ibid. 23d March, 1861.]

Mr. Mirés has been transferred from the prison of Mazas to the Conciergerie, which is in a central position, and consequently more convenient for the judicial inquiry. * * * *

The Moniteur of the 5th instant contains A REPORT ADDRESSED BY THE MINISTER OF JUSTICE TO THE EMPEROR, on the subject of the affairs of Mr. Mirés.

The minister mentions the reports which have been prevalent, and according to which Mr. Mirés had known how to create for himself, *by a suspicious generosity,* protectors sufficiently powerful to shield him from the chastisement of justice. The reports also asserted that the evil was *so general and so great* that the Government, at the risk of saving the guilty parties, had resolved on allowing the affair to drop, in order to AVOID SCANDALS WHOSE RESULTS WOULD BE INCALCULABLE, rather than lay bare the moral ulcers caused by this corruption. [Ibid. 23d March, 1861.]

That there has been a certain degree of winnowing or sifting out of accomplices associated with the Imperial *entourage*, is no longer a question. Their liabilities have been discharged from the Imperial private exchequer, and the grand delinquent being thus brought to the foreground (without any other important character to divide the spectator's eye), the exhibition will be duly opened. He is in close confinement, and a sharp surveillance is exercised that he does nothing to cheat the law of its victim. I learn from those personally intimate with him that his courage does not give way, so that whenever the hour comes that he is placed face to face with his accusers, he is determined to cry aloud and spare not. Prince Polignac,* who married his daughter, is in a pitiable plight. [Ibid. Mar., 1861.]

So many distinguished members of the Imperial *entourage* are, it seems, shown by the books to have received bribes— or as they are picturesquely called here *pots de vin*—from Mr. Mirés to obtain concessions, &c., that the disclosures would compel the Emperor to dismiss some of his most trustworthy councillors. It is said that the sum expended in bribery, during the last four years, amounts to no less than 13,000,000 francs......... When, by the care of M. De Germiny, all (or nearly all) danger has been averted from the sacred heads of those *nearest to the throne*, then, probably, the law will be allowed to step in and deal severely with smaller people......
Besides the million of the late King of Westphalia (Prince Jerome, uncle of the Emperor), the Princess Mathilde, (his sister) is to be cleared of a debt amounting to £20,000.

As to the amount of Count de Morny's (the Emperor's illegitimate brother's) liabilities in this most scandalous business— that will probably never at any time during the present regime be known; for his misdemeanors of this kind are so bound up with a still higher person, [the Empress] that the determination is to keep him free from all accusation of any sort whatever..... Morny is the object of universal attack just now, and at the last Council, before the Emperor himself, a member who was present stated in my hearing that M. de Persigny, staring M. de Morny in the face, said:

"Yes! the time has come when *all dishonest men* must be made to suffer!"

I repeat it, the effect of all this is tremendous, and makes former scandals such as the Teste and Cubières or even the Praslin affairs seem very small. [N. Y. Tribune, 18th March, 1861.]

Judgment was given on the 11th inst., in the affairs of Mirés and Solar. Both were condemned to five years imprisonment, and 3000 francs fine. [N. Y. Herald, 24th July, 1861.]

This punishment was merely nominal—never enforced: and was simply a concession to public opinion.

1861, Feb. 11.—The Claimant wrote to the French Minister of Foreign Affairs, Mr. Thouvenel, through the French Ambassador M. Mercier, at Washington, requesting another private audience of the Emperor, which elicited no notice.

*This miscreant passed two years in the United States preceding the rebellion, engaged in organizing the "Knights of the Golden Circle," and afterwards served as a Confederate Brigadier-General in the field.

1860, Aug. 24.—The Claimant wrote to Count Fialin de Persigny, French Ambassador at London, in the same sense, and with the same result, which letter is believed to have occasioned the world-renowned arrest of Mr. Mirés, and the threatened prosecution, by the Emperor, of Count de Morny, &c., *for speculating in Mines*, as above detailed.

Interview of the Claimant with Prince Napoleon.

1861, Aug. 5.—After a previous interview with Prince Napoleon Bonaparte, then in Washington, U. S., who promised to deliver to the Emperor, *without fail*, a letter from the Claimant soliciting a further audience; such a letter was written and delivered to the Prince at the French Embassy at Washington, but in like manner elicited no notice.

A number of other affidavits, reinforcing most of the previously related facts, are on file at Washington—whose quotation would only overload these pages. They are accordingly omitted.

Numerous letters from the Claimant to various official personages of the French Government are also omitted for the like reason. For the most part they enclosed letters to the Emperor soliciting another audience with a view to a settlement of the Claim, but as they held out but faint hopes of any thing else which could be successfully pillaged from him without payment, were naturally received with contumelious neglect. Not a syllable of response was ever vouchsafed to them.

Letters of the Claimant not noticed by the French Government.

To the Minister of the French Marine, Paris, 6 June, 1854.
"   "   "   "   Havre, 4 July, 1854.
"   "   "   "   Paris, 3 Oct., 1856.
"   "   "   "   Paris, 15 Oct., 1856.
To the Emperor, Paris, 3 Oct., 1856.
"   "   "   26 Jan., 1857.

Ditto not printed in this volume.

To the French Ambassador at London, Phila., 24 Aug., 1860.
To the Emperor through Mr. Mercier, Ambassador, Phila., 11 Feb., 1861.
To the Emperor through Prince Napoleon, Wash., 5 Aug., 1861.

Testimonial to the Character of the Claimant.

PHILADELPHIA, 22d Feb., 1866.

SIR:—The undersigned, from their knowledge of the character and attainments of Mr. Robert A. Parrish, Jr., of this city, who is understood to hold a large claim against the Government of France, respectfully represent, that they believe him to be incapable of preferring such a claim unless the same were based upon just and tenable grounds; and that in their judgment the Government of the United States would be derelict in duty towards its citizens were it to withhold from him any needful facility for the settlement thereof.

With distinguished consideration, your obedient servants,

MORTON McMICHAEL,
Mayor of Philadelphia.
DAVID PAUL BROWN,
Counsellor at Law.
WM. B. THOMAS,
U. S. Collector, Phila.
A. J. PERKINS,
Secretary Board of Trade.
JOHN RUDD,
Com. U. S. Navy.
E. J. LEWIS,
No. 126 Chestnut st., Phila.
ALEXANDER HENRY,
Late Mayor of Philadelphia.
R. RUNDLE SMITH,
Counsellor at Law.
W. S. LEWIS,
No. 126 Chestnut st., Phila.
GEORGE W. BIDDLE,
Counsellor at Law.
&c., &c., &c.

To His Excellency, W. H. SEWARD,
Secretary of State, Washington, D. C.

ARGUMENT OF THE CLAIMANT

UPON THE

INTERNATIONAL LAW OF THE CASE.

As it would be fatiguing to reïterate the argument embodied in the Claimant's letter to the Department of State, of December 18, 1865 (ante p. 113), the conclusions of law therein established will be adopted as a point of departure for the further argument now submitted.

That letter demonstrated upon the written admissions of the French Government the precise amount of this claim (in other words, that it was a claim for "liquidated damages"); the consideration upon which it was based; the date at which it was payable; the fact that it was long overdue, and that justice had been denied the Claimant through unprincipled evasions and prolonged delay. That delay now (1869) attains to the unreasonable length of some fifteen years.

It was likewise therein established that the claim was to have been secured by a written Treaty with the French Government; that this Treaty was wholly or partially completed by the Minister of the French Marine, in pursuance of the Emperor's Parole, and that it was subsequently embezzled, or fraudulently withheld.

The principles of law considered in that letter were those of the lex loci (the Civil law of France) and the parallel or identical principles of the English common law which govern the interpretation of contracts.

The present argument will discuss the rights and remedies of the Claimant, and the power and obligations of his government in the premises, in their relations with the International Code, or "Law of Nations;" whose principles wielding equal authority both in Europe and America, will define and determine the case.

In the course of this discussion it will be necessary to ascertain:

First. Whether International Law and usage justify one government in enforcing against another the claims of its citizens; and,

Second. Under what circumstances such an enforcement is deemed warrantable.

The language of the distinguished authors cited in the sequel will manifest that the exercise of such authority is an inherent and unquestioned prerogative of all governments, and has been familiar in practice from immemorial time. It is a right indeed, which is not only strongly inculcated and sustained by written doctrine, but has the concurrent sanction of long established usage and *unanimous consent.* It will be found to have been incorporated from the beginning amongst the very fundamental principles of the International Code, and is consequently less open to question and theoretical doubt than perhaps any other postulate.

By all writers upon the Jus Gentium—A WRONG DONE TO A CITIZEN IS REGARDED AS A WRONG DONE TO THE NATION OF WHICH HE IS A PART:—and it is immaterial whether the wrong be addressed to his person or to his estate; whether he be imprisoned and maltreated, or whether his property simply be taken away. Nor is the distinction essential as to whether this be accomplished by fraud or by violence; by the subjects of a foreign Sovereign or by the Sovereign himself.

De Vattel, the renowned French jurist (equal in authority to any writer of his age), and still quoted with veneration in the Courts of France, tells us (Law of Nations, London, 8vo, 1797, ch. v, sec. 63, p. 160): "Justice is the basis of all society;" and (ch. vi, sec. 72, p. 162): "If a Sovereign, who might keep his subjects within the rules of justice and peace, suffers them to injure a foreign nation, *either in its body or its members,* he does no less injury to that nation than if he injured it himself." This proposition may of course be urged a fortiori, if the Sovereign himself be the perpetrator of the injury, as is the fact in the present case. In the same spirit, the noted German publicist Klüber (Europäisches Volkerrecht, Schaffhausen, p.

231,) asseverates, that—"A State may be injured in two ways: either *directly*, by a violation of right affecting its collective capacity; or *indirectly*, by a violation of the right of the individual *to whom it owes protection, in return for his allegiance.*"

The same opinion, in ipsissimis verbis, will be found in Phillimore's Com. on International Law, London, 8vo, 1855, Vol. III, p. 10, from whose acknowledged high standing with the Courts of England, those Courts may be regarded as acquiescing with the Government and Courts both of Germany and France in the proposition in question. So also our American Kent declares (Coms. N. Y., 8vo, 1826, Vol. I, p. 46: Art. Law of Nations): "An injury, either done or *threatened*, to the perfect rights of a nation *or of any of its members*, and susceptible of no other redress, is a just cause of war. The injury may consist not only in the direct violation of personal or political rights, *but in wrongfully withholding what is due*, or in the refusal of a reasonable reparation for injuries committed."

If, then, the principle be accepted, as beyond dispute, that for a wrong perpetrated, or even so much as threatened, by a Foreign State, the Government of the victim may intervene in his defence:—by a further reference to the same code, the special conditions may be ascertained which render such intervention proper and justifiable. It will likewise be made apparent that when intervention has been decided upon, its exercise will be accompanied by force, if (in the judgment of the injured nation) force be deemed necessary to the ends of justice. The measure of that force is limited by circumstances. If by making reprisals, or the mere seizure of the property of the offending nation (or of its subjects), an adequate indemnity can be realized, no further violence will be resorted to. Nor is its employment to this extent held to be such an aggression as to furnish the defendant nation with cause of war. In case, however, indemnity by means of reprisals is found to be impracticable, or inadequate to satisfy the demands of justice, war may be justly waged until those demands are appeased. The ample and solid grounds of reason adduced in behalf of these doctrines are embodied in the fact, that not only is a citizen destitute of the power to cope with offending nations, but even if otherwise, its exercise by him would be clearly a contravention of the general weal. It would involve the world in discord. Hence, as his allegiance is a duty which is exacted by his Government, so his Government in return for the concession is bound to vindicate and defend him against foreign aggression. On these points the legal authorities speak in the following decisive terms:

De Vattel declares [Ibid. p. 285, section 347,] "We may make reprisals against a nation not only *for the actions of its Sovereign*, but also for those of his subjects, and this may take place when the State or Sovereign participates in the act of his subject and takes it upon himself!"

According to Phillimore, "It is to be borne in mind, that individuals have committed the defence of themselves to the States, of which they are members, and having done so, they are not entitled to redress their own injuries, or (to use a common but expressive phrase,) to take the law into their own hands." [Ibid. Vol. III, p. 10.]

Grotius, in his Rights of War and Peace, folio, Lond., 1738, asserts, "Reprisals amongst divers nations may be enforced where right is denied; which may be assumed, not only *when judgment cannot within a reasonable time be obtained* against a malefactor or debtor, but also . . . . . when sentence shall pass [in the tribunals] plainly against right." [Book III, chap. II, sec. IV, p. 542.]

The same opinion will be found reiterated and affirmed by all of the following distinguished authors, viz:

Baron Puffendorf, art. Reprisals.
Bartolus, De Repressaliis, Quæst. V, § 3, No. 9.
Innocent and Panor, in Can. VIII.
Dominic Soto, Lib. III, Quæst. IV, Art. V.
Jacob de Canibus, in Can. I.
Fulgosius and Salicetus, IV De Injuriis.
Sylvest. Verb Represalia.
Guido Papa, Quæst. XXXII.
Francisc Victoria, De Jure Belli, num. 41.
De Martens and De Cussy, Recucil de Traités, Lib. VIII, ch. 2, p. 260.
Valin, Com. sur L'ord de la Marine, Lib. III, t. 9.
Zouch, De Jure Feciali, p. 120.

Manning, Law of Nations, ch. III.
Wheaton, Elements, I, Part IV, chap. 2.

By the eleventh paragraph, moreover, of section eighth of the first article of the Constitution of the United States, the right of making reprisals for the express purpose and in the very sense above set forth is vested in the American Congress, viz: "Congress shall have power to declare war, grant letters of marque and reprisal, and make rules concerning captures by land or water."

Under this clause the jurisdiction of the Federal Government in the present case attaches.

But Phillimore says, "It most commonly happens that reprisals are resorted to for the purpose of redressing injuries inflicted upon the rights of individuals..... An injury committed upon one of his subjects, for which justice has been *plainly denied or unreasonably delayed*, warrants a Sovereign in issuing letters of marque or reprisal, &c..... The injury may be of an active kind, that is, accompanied with actual force and violence, or it may be of a passive kind, i. e. withholding OR REFUSING TO PAY A DEBT JUSTLY DUE, for which the creditor has not been able to obtain justice in the Courts of Law of the debtor's country.... Moreover, it must be, res minime dubia, in which justice has been denied, and [if the debt of a subject] it must have been absolutely denied by all the tribunals of the country *before which the cause could be brought*, and *also by the Sovereign in the last resort.*" P. 14.

De Vattel, the French Jurisconsult, says, "But in order perfectly to understand this article it must be observed that if, EVEN IN A DISPUTABLE CASE, OUR ADVERSARY REFUSES TO PURSUE OR ARTFULLY EVADES the necessary steps for bringing the matter to the proof: if he does not *candidly and sincerely* accede to some pacific mode of terminating the dispute, *especially if he is foremost* in adopting violent measures,* he gives justice to our cause which before was problematical." [Ibid. p. 284.]

In the same sense, Phillimore continues, "No country has better understood both the theory and practice of reprisals than the United States of North America." [Vol. III, p. 33.]

---
* See the particulars of the attempts to assassinate the Claimant. (Pages 58, 59, 73 and 74, ante.)

And quotes in illustration the opinions and proceedings of General Jackson against France in 1836. Jackson's opinion is set forth by Wheaton in enforcement of like views, as follows: "It is a well settled principle of the international code, that where one nation owes another *a liquidated debt*, which it refuses or neglects to pay, the aggrieved party may seize on property belonging to the other, its citizens or subjects, sufficient to pay the debt, without giving just cause of war. I recommend that a law be passed authorizing reprisals upon French property in case provision shall not be made for the payment of the debt, at the approaching session of the French Chambers." [Elements, Vol. II, p. 508, Note 168.]

It thus appears that the conditions which must attach to a claim to entitle it to international redress are two:

First.—The claim, whatever its original character, must be for what is called "liquidated damages," or in other words for a fixed and definite sum of money.

Second.—Justice must have been denied or unfairly administered in the Courts of the offending country, (if any there be holding jurisdiction of the subject matter,) and must afterwards have been denied by the Sovereign himself. *But unreasonable delay by the Sovereign in awarding justice is tantamount to its positive denial.*

When these conditions are fulfilled nothing more is requisite to entitle the Claimant to the authoritative vindication of his country. Usage of course requires that he should solicit that vindication; whereupon his Government by undoubted law, either by reprisals or by open war, may redress the wrong. No exercise of force, however, can possibly be necessary in the present case, for upon the suggestion of the Government of the United States, that a settlement is expected of France, the money will be paid. To gratify his ministry in pillaging an American of a few millions of francs, the Emperor would scarcely expose his people or his still more precious dynasty to the accidents of an unjust and an unnecessary war.

Now as to the first condition, it is enough to say that the definite amount of this claim is conceded at all hands. No dispute has arisen, nor is pretended to exist as to fifteen millions of francs, with interest since August 15th, 1854, being the true amount. It was payable when any part of the Auriferous territory indicated by the Claimant should be realized by France.

By Mr. Fould's letter of 27th June, 1854, above quoted, [p. 33] it is confessed that a vast portion of the territory in question was realized before the date of that letter. From such time therefore the claim bears interest; but to simplify dates, the 15th day of August following, (the birthday of Napoleon I,) is allowed by the claimant to be the time from which interest is to be computed, as that day was officially set apart as a holiday to celebrate the French intrusion into the gold fields. [Vide Official Report, 18 Oct., 1858, p. 104, ante.] The claim therefore as to date, amount, and other circumstances is incontestably a claim for "liquidated damages."

As to the second condition—the correspondence shows that this is a claim not upon a subject but upon the Emperor and Government of France, and cannot therefore be heard in her tribunals.

According to Wheaton;—by the law of France foreigners, "Who have established their domicile in the country.... .. are entitled to all civil rights:—amongst others to that of suing in the local tribunals as French subjects. Under other circumstances these tribunals have jurisdiction where foreigners are parties in the *following cases only* :

"1. When the contract is made between foreigners and French subjects.

"2. In *commercial matters* on all contracts made in France where the parties, if foreigners, *have elected a domicile*.

"3. Where foreigners voluntarily submit their controversies [with each other] to the decision of the French tribunals, by waiving a plea to their jurisdiction.

"*In all other cases* where foreigners, not domiciled, are concerned, the French tribunals decline jurisdiction *even when the contract is made in France*." [Elements of International Law, Boston, 8vo, 1855, p. 200.]

The Claimant never sought or acquired domicile in France. The Claim as already stated is against the Emperor and Government, not against a subject of France. The Courts of

France demonstrably hold no jurisdiction of it. But even if they did, those Courts specially represent the Emperor. They are created expressly to exert and uphold his authority against all comers. Although in petty disputes among his subjects they are permitted to dispense an even-handed justice; where he himself is a party such an expectation would be chimerical! His Majesty *is* the Court. As well might the Claimant constitute himself a Court and adjudicate the Claim!

But its adjudication by the French Courts is unnecessary on other grounds.

It is a maxim of law, that in matters of contract, if conditions precedent exist whose fulfillment is necessary to entitle a party to a recovery, proof of such fulfillment is incumbent upon him. But it is equally a settled maxim of law, that if before the time of such fulfillment the other party declares that he intends to abandon or violate the contract, or does abandon or violate it, the fulfillment of such conditions precedent becomes unnecessary. [Vide Starkie on Evid., Vol. II, p. 1188, and Bank *vs*. Horner, 1 Peters, p. 464.]

Even if the Courts of France then actually held jurisdiction of this matter, (which they do not) and if they were allowed to be disinterested and just, (which they are not,) still the principles of law just enunciated entirely discharge the Claimant from all necessity of a preliminary appeal to them for justice, in order to entitle him to diplomatic aid. The Emperor had flatly abandoned and violated the contract in advance!

That violation was made perfect by the Emperor, (speaking through his Imperial Minister of State, Mr. Fould,) in the letter just referred to, of June 27th, 1854 [ante p. 83]. It had been previously perfected by His Majesty's "artful evasion," (which Vattel denominates *fraud*,) expressed in the letter of the Imperial Grand Chamberlain of June 19th, 1854, [ante p. 33]. It was still further perfected by the "evasive" letter of his Private Secretary Mocquard [ante p. 53]. And finally, it was rendered *plus-perfect* by His Majesty's personal violation of his promises of a future audience, as given to the Claimant in the Palace of the Tuileries, December 28th, 1856 [ante pp. 48 and 49]. Even if all this were insufficient, the Emperor's refusal of justice, was virtually repeated and enforced again and again by the sturdy silence of his Government in withholding all notice or reply to the reiterated letters of the Claimant, covering the long interval of the past fifteen years! [vide p. 142] delay in granting justice being held by all the legal authorities to be tantamount to its refusal.

Besides, look at the aggravations which accompany this case! What Emperor with half his knowledge of the world, aware as was Napoleon III of the insatiable rapacity of his Ministers, would have flung a friendless and defenceless stranger a prey to their demoniacal wiles! Not to have kept a guardian eye over his life and interests implies an absolute destitution of honor and humanity. It shows that so long as these Shylocks maintain him with their impious spoil, he would callously see them sack the four corners of the earth, and if possible the seventh Heaven itself.

Moreover, instead of some little show of respect to that originality of mind which had opened to the philosophers of France such infinite themes of study, to her statesmen such noble fields of ambition, and to the Government generally (particularly to the reigning family) such legitimate and exhaustless sources of useful and honorable distinction, all the Claimant has realized has been heavy pecuniary losses and the most baleful and brutal persecutions. No opulent traveler, fallen amongst Bedoueens, was ever more pitilessly pillaged. For his very life the Claimant is indebted not to their forbearance but to his own unwearied vigilance. So far from permitting him to realize a fragment of that well earned credit to which he is here entitled, he was even exposed to intellectual privations of the cruellest kind. He was amongst other things excluded not only from the [Libraries of Paris, but also by low Jewish and Romanish defamations from two of the learned Societies and Libraries of America!! [vide p. 59, ante.] To the French Government these wretched triumphs are easy of achievement; armed and skilled as it ever is in the use of falsehoods and slanders that would slay the Archangels: and deeply experienced in that dire credulity of men, which, upon official authority, *can credit anything whatever—but the truth.*

142

Hence, when the late President of the United States united with the emissaries of France in maligning the Claimant, perhaps the success of such infamy should cease to be surprising. He is, of course, a malefactor and a caitiff, saturated with every species of infamy, and should he humbly pray for justice, is unworthy of heed. Such is the logic of a larcenous Jew!

Were it not impertinent to this argument, the Claimant could readily demonstrate that the cyclopean fraud upon the Treasury of France, above detailed, of one hundred and twenty millions of dollars was perpetrated by Mirés in the name of the Claimant, and by a forgery of his authority; but of the fruits of which he realized not even a centime! It could also be readily demonstrated that from these African mines alone (wrought by thousands of captives) could this tremendous sum of money possibly have been derived:—a sum, surpassing the aggregated larcenies of man since the creation, and representing an insatiable audacity to which Jews alone are equal. Nor satisfied with even this, could they spare the Claimant until they had cut from him a pound of flesh nearest the heart:—the very merit and originality of his enterprise having been ravished from him! Drunk with arrogance (and regardless of their grotesque fit) they have mentally equipped themselves in his "old clothes!!"*

Mr. Buchanan, who was a pretty good lawyer, (probably from a conviction that all the foregoing grounds of hostility were untenable,) finally sought to baffle and defeat the Claimant by a different plea. There has lately grown up in the U. S. Department of State as a measure of convenience, a usage, (not sanctioned or authorized by any law,) of refusing to *all claims on Foreign Governments arising out of contracts* the notice

---

* The claimant would here state that the reflections contained in this volume against Jews and Roman Catholics refer only to Cardinals, Bishops, Rabbis, chiefs, and representative leaders, who are not believed to be better than other men, but who by the common law of humanity if addicted to pure selfishness sooner or later perish by it. Gamblers as a class illustrate this,—whether gamblers in money, religion or politics—as in the last particular, our late rebellion has abundantly evinced, and especially in the case of the late Roman Catholic Bishop of Chicago. Mr. Mirés and his gang are further illustrations. If the Emperor was aware of what they have selfishly deprived him (ante, p. 99) he would utterly exterminate them.

or advocacy of the Department. This is well understood to mean commercial contracts, whose name is legion. Taking this false ground, Mr. Buchanan renounced the imperious duty of seeing justice administered here, encouraged by the hope that in the then approaching rebellion the Republic must inevitably perish, and that no nationality could thereafter espouse the claim. This theory failed. Mr. Seward, however, struggled to resuscitate it. [Vide his letter, ante p. 124]. The Claim cannot be defeated by such means. It is not a commercial contract. It belongs to a totally different category. It has no commercial characteristics whatsoever. It embodies none of the generic features of the cases thus classified by the Department. The issue here is directly with the Emperor. the head of the State. All negotiation with his subordinates was refused ab initio; and for the then clearly expressed purpose of stripping the subject of the very ambiguities in which Mr. Buchanan and Mr. Hunter have so strenuously labored to involve it. Instead of a commercial bargain wherein there is some material thing to be sold and delivered, and wherein money is to be paid in some specific ratio with the quantity and quality of such material—(all which matters commercial courts could adjudge)—there was in this case neither material nor sale. It was information only which was imparted to the Emperor; scientific information whose exalted import no ordinary legal tribunal could presume to measure. Statesmen only could appreciate its prodigious moment. And in this precise sense it was accepted and estimated by His Majesty. He deemed it the appropriate subject of a national Treaty, and (as has been shown) proffered the same to the Claimant for his better security. The Emperor's Parole alone was asked for; the infamy of its violation not being thought within the bounds of possibility! The Treaty, however, was gratuitously and munificently superadded. Thus understood, it is quite as iniquitous to falsify the nature of the Claim by denouncing it as a mere commercial contract, or upon any of the other grounds above alleged, to deny it the advocacy of the Government, as it was to perpetrate a forgery upon the Claimant's papers, or to resent his appeals for justice by criminal designs upon his life.

It may furthermore be added, that no Secretary of State (unless he means to bring the purity of his motives in question) can wisely venture to abrogate those rights conferred upon a citizen by the Constitution of the United States; much less under the guise of "business rules" to substitute for the law his individual caprice. The functions of the Departments of the Government and the rights of the people to protection are alike established and defined by law. It is enough, therefore, to repeat that the law not only of this country but of all countries, the JUS GENTIUM itself, most unequivocally endows a citizen (wronged as the Claimant has been) with the right to a just, bold and thorough going vindication. To withhold it would be either a tyrannical abuse or a most questionable error. But to place the iniquity of this pretended "rule" in a still clearer light, it can be shown that even if the Claimant's Treaty with France were a mere "commercial contract," the rule in question could have no just application here, because it is *ex post facto*. It was instituted *after* the origin of the Claim, with the intent and purpose to defeat it, and is therefore a nullity. And if one Secretary can *at pleasure* institute such a rule, another (equally at pleasure) may repeal it; particularly as it is entirely unsupported by any statutory enactment. Such a rule would in fact repeal all laws which relate to the subject, and operate the total annihilation of international remedies. If one class of claims can be thus annihilated so can another And if, when a Treaty with the French Emperor is in question, a Secretary can affect to believe, as Mr. Seward did, [Letter of Nov. 27, 1865, p. 111, ante,] that it is a mere private bargain with Mr. Louis Bonaparte, and that Mr. Louis Bonaparte is a French subject—(not the head of the State)—he not only renounces all allegiance to law or even to veracity, but sets at defiance the principles of common sense. Argument upon such ground is impossible.

If, then, upon the foregoing data the Government of the United States does not interfere in vindication of this Claim, a serious question is presented as to the worth or value of our entire diplomatic machinery. 't can be regarded as little else than a hollow pretence, useless for practical purposes, and but a pleasing and pompous display of national imbecility.

Nay worse than this, it becomes a snare for the lives as well as for the interests of the people. For wo betide the individual who in a Claim of this magnitude should, without a sponsor for his life, dare to ask for justice of a Government like France. [Witness the fate of Mr. Morley in a much smaller affair, ante p. 72.]

It has been hinted in mousing whispers that France has realized no gold, and that inasmuch as gold was the main object of the negotiation it would be inequitable to insist on her payment of so large a sum. This (as has been abundantly shown above) is either the language of unintentional error, or of conscious and intentional falsification. France without compulsion will pay nothing—Gold or no Gold. If she held the proposed Territory or any part of it, she was to pay for it without regard to the amount of gold, or even to the fact that any gold whatever should be realized. [Ante p. 25.] It would have been wholly immaterial therefore to the equity of this case (since vast portions of the territory have been seized and held by France,) if gold had not been found. It would be unjust in the extreme therefore to throw the onus probandi of this point upon the Claimant, particularly as every effort of the most subtle craft has been exerted by France to conceal the infinite mineral wealth of this region. But if (as the Claimant has proved by the official admissions of the Empire, pp. 93, 94, 102, 103, 104, 121, &c.,) gold has been found, and even to a prodigious and unexampled extent, there is no remaining vestige of palliation, either for the fraud or the base ingratitude of the Emperor. To make that fraud still more glaring, it is enough to say, that the embezzlement or confiscation of the Claimant's rights, was in fact consummated in December, 1853, *even before the departure of the French Expedition to Africa, and accordingly before the existence or receipt of gold had possibly been brought to the proof!!*

This is established by the refusal of the Minister of the French Marine before the middle of that month, (after clutching the Memorial of the Claimant,) either to give him further audience or to deliver the promised Treaty; also by the infamous seizure in the mails of his American letters and remittances, thereby expelling him from France; furthermore, by the abject falsehood of Mr. Fould as uttered to the Claimant at the audience of the 16th of that month, [vide p. 24, ante,] and this although the approving report of Mr. Ducos was in his hands, and the executive policy and Imperial Decrees of France in full operation! To that policy and those Decrees Mr. Fould, as Prime Minister of the Emperor, had assisted to give energy, and shape, and life! [Vide Decrees of 8d Dec., &c., ante p. 99.] It is therefore the very wantonness of falsification to pretend that the non-receipt of gold (even if true) constituted any part of the reason for this fraud. Holland and other Governments moreover would have paid the Claimant many millions of francs for the same Proposition. [Hon. S. L. Gouverneur's affidavit, p. 45.] He was in treaty with two of them to that effect, and was only thwarted by the spies of France. He can get that sum for his Proposition now, if placed in statu quo ante negotitionem. But this will never be. The Emperor has declared (as we have seen, p. 98) that France will never relinquish her grasp upon this inestimable territory. On the contrary, whilst she clings to it with positively a frantic tenacity, she pretends to decry its value, and compensates the Claimant only with slanders, with murderous persecutions, and with the protean falsehoods of her ubiquitous spies.

In conclusion, it may be confidently asserted that there is nothing in the Law of France, nothing in the Law of the United States, nothing in the Law of nations, and nothing in considerations of policy, either public or particular, which should bar a demand for the payment of this Claim. On the contrary, from all these sources the most cogent instances can be derived to sanction and justify it. Moreover, Justice exacts it. If such a demand be made the Claim will be paid, not otherwise. The Jews (both in and out of office) will bluster and threaten of course, will open the batteries of all their subsidized presses upon it, will talk of the national honor of France, (as though they personated it,) and will offer in bribes over half the debt—but if it be positively demanded it will be positively paid. As to fighting in vindication of a Theft, the proposition is preposterous. France single handed will in no event fight with this country, even with a good cause of quarrel, much less in such a degraded larcenous cause as this. The late President, Mr. Buchanan, asserted the contrary, *but he knew better*, and had an interest in his mendacity. It is a mournful commentary indeed upon the honesty of the French Government, and upon the past inefficiency of our own diplomatic system, that an American should have been the victim of such a colossal outrage, and that under the conniving smiles of his Presidential and Diplomatic representatives it should have enjoyed such prolonged and such absolute impunity.

But enough: no one of ordinary understanding (always excepting those mercenaries, late of the Department of State, who from virtuous and purely disinterested motives forged and misrepresented the Records of the Claimant) can peruse the testimony accompanying this Claim and indulge even the affectation of a doubt as to its unequivocal integrity; nor can they doubt the equal right and the duty of his Government to extort from the French Government its honorable liquidation. Moreover, the Emperor has vain-gloriously declared that his Ministers are not "thieves who desire to cheat," but on the contrary, are "honest men." [Ante p. 71.] Let him be taken at his word. Let this claim be honestly paid, and these assertions verified. Then perhaps the world can credit him. At all events it is indubitable, that if it be not those servile Jews, from the kennels of Europe, still surrounding and upholding the Imperial Throne, who, through Mr. Mirés, have defrauded both the Claimant and the Emperor in the premises, and who by the Claimant's assassination are still seeking to silence his voice forever, then to Napoleon III (this mighty modern Cæsar), alone belong the infamy and the guilt—as well as *all the profit*—of these most ignoble wrongs.

R. A. PARRISH, Jr.,
No. 1305 Arch Street.